A D
American Presidents
Vol. 1

Presidents 1-24 George Washington to
Grover Cleveland

By Michael W. Simmons

Table of Contents

Part One: The Era of Good Feelings (The Founding Fathers)

One
George Washington
(1732-1799)

Time in Office

1789-1797

George Washington was born February 22, 1732, on a modest tobacco farm in Westmoreland County, Virginia, to Augustine and Mary Ball Washington. He was the oldest of the couple's six children. By a previous marriage, Augustine Washington had two elder sons, one of whom, Lawrence, was a great influence on Washington as a child. When George Washington was eleven, his father died, leaving him heir to his property, including a farm, some acreage of land, and eleven slaves. Because Washington was forced to assume responsibility for his family's farm when he was only a child, he was not allowed to follow in his brother's footsteps and go to England to receive a gentleman's education, and for most of his adult life he was prone to feelings of insecurity and inadequacy regarding his education. Washington attended a few local schools until the age of fifteen, and pursued a lifelong course of rigorous, self-imposed study.

Washington's career prospects were bolstered considerably when his brother Lawrence married Nancy Fairfax, daughter of Colonel William Fairfax, one of the wealthiest landowners in Virginia. Colonel Fairfax took a liking to his son-in-law's young brother, and gave him the run of his extensive library. As a teenager, Washington divided his time between his father's farm and Lawrence's Potomac estates of Little Hunting Creek and Mount Vernon. With the assistance of Colonel Fairfax, Washington took up property surveying as a profession, traveling deep into the Shenandoah Valley to divide the unsettled

American countryside into saleable tracts of land. This would enable Washington to assure his own fortune by making lucrative land investments.

By 1752, both Lawrence Washington and his young daughter had died, leaving George Washington heir to his properties at the age of twenty. That same year, he joined the colonial militia and entered the first phase of his military career as an adjutant in the North American theater of the Seven Years' War, known in American history as the French and Indian War. Over the course of the campaign Washington traveled throughout what was then the western American frontier, as part of the effort to drive the French out of the unsettled territories claimed by Britain. Washington, who had hoped for an illustrious career in the English army, grew frustrated with the limited prospects afforded to colonial officers, and accordingly resigned his commission at the war's conclusion. The seeds of his eventual discontent with English rule were planted during this period, and the military experience he had gained in the war would make him the natural choice to lead the American army during the Revolutionary War.

Washington was married on January 6, 1759, to Martha Dandridge Custis, a wealthy widow with two children from her first marriage. Washington was very close to Martha's daughter, Patsy, who suffered from severe epilepsy, though he was often frustrated by Patsy's brother, Jack, whom Washington considered spoiled and lazy. Patsy Custis's death as a young teenager affected Washington deeply. Upon the death of her first husband, Martha Washington had inherited half his estate, with half set aside for her children's inheritance. Washington was in charge of managing his step-son's estate, but he could not sell any part of it, nor could he free any of the Custis slaves, though on his deathbed he would make the highly unusual and controversial decision to order his own slaves freed after his wife's death.

For over a decade Washington lived a quiet but active life as a family man and a farmer, attending meetings of the House of Burgesses and acting as a justice of the peace. He was present for Patrick Henry's famous speech in the Virginia assembly in which he proclaimed, "give me liberty or give me death," a response to the Stamp Act in 1765. By 1768, Washington had recognized the inevitability of war with England and had begun to prepare for the possibility that his military services would be called upon in defense of his country. In 1774, Washington was sent to Philadelphia as one of seven Virginia delegates to the first Continental Congress. In 1775, the second Continental Congress unanimously appointed him general of the new Continental Army. As a Virginian, his appointment satisfied the delegates from the southern colonies, while his reputation for selflessness and lack of personal ambition reassured other members of the congress that there was little danger of his attempting to seize domestic power at the war's end.

The difficulty of Washington's task as commander-in-chief of the American army can scarcely be overstated. While the British were fielding professionally trained troops, Washington's men were volunteers, untrained, lacking in military discipline, with few experienced officers among them. As Congress was unable to levy taxes, it had difficulty paying or equipping the soldiers, who found themselves marching without boots, slaughtering pack animals for food, and fighting with farm implements. Thousands died or deserted. Historians credit Washington's personal leadership qualities, even more than his military talents, with holding the army together in the face of the odds stacked against them. At the war's end in 1783, Washington returned to the Continental Congress to resign his commission. European observers expected Washington to use his position as general of a victorious army to have himself declared king of the newly independent American states, and were astonished when he instead returned to his estate of Mount Vernon to live as a farmer for the next four years.

In May of 1787, Washington was appointed as one of five Virginia delegates to the first Constitutional Convention, where he emerged as the sole figure capable of uniting the northern and southern states. Due to his experiences as head of the army, Washington was a staunch proponent of federalist principles of government, which would later place him at odds with fellow Virginians such as Thomas Jefferson and James Madison. His election in 1789 as the first president of the United States was unanimous, due to the respect he commanded both at home and abroad and the legitimacy which his name lent to the fledgling government.

Washington was inaugurated in New York on April 30, 1789, with John Adams of Massachusetts serving as his vice-president. Reluctant to abandon his private life in Virginia and return to public service, Washington would serve as president for only two four-year terms, thereby establishing a precedent that all future presidents would observe until Franklin Delano Roosevelt was elected for a third term in 1940. The sections of the Constitution outlining the role of the American president were written with Washington in mind, and more than any other president, he defined the office for generations to come. Washington's first cabinet was comprised of Thomas Jefferson, serving as secretary of state, Alexander Hamilton as the treasury secretary, Henry Knox as secretary of war, and attorney general Edmund Randolph. During Washington's second presidential term, the first political parties began to emerge upon the American political landscape: on the one side, the Federalists, who advocated strong central government and were suspected by their opponents of being secret monarchists, and on the other, Democratic-Republicans, who envisioned the United States as a confederacy of sovereign city-states bound together for mutual defense but otherwise self-governing. By the end of Washington's second term, the rivalry between the two parties had turned bitter, and Washington expressed his fears that partisanship would destroy the fragile young republic. Despite being urged to do, he chose not to pursue a third term in office, and returned to Mount Vernon in 1797 to devote himself to farming in his retirement.

Public life would not leave Washington behind, however. Visitors traveled from all over Virginia, and all over the country, to visit Mount Vernon and pay their respects to General Washington. Washington rarely found himself able to enjoy a quiet meal alone with his family without at least one uninvited guest being present, and the financial strain of feeding so many visitors proved considerable. In 1798, when the nation faced the prospect of war with France, Washington was once again appointed commander in chief of the American army. He would hold the office until his death the following year.

In December of 1799, after riding the rounds of Mount Vernon for several hours in the snow and rain, Washington took a chill which quickly developed into an infection. After two days in bed, he died, attended by his wife and servants. He was buried in a vault on his Mount Vernon estate.

Memorable quote:

"In offering to you, my countrymen, these counsels of an old and affectionate friend, I dare not hope they will make the strong and lasting impression I could wish; that they will control the usual current of the passions, or prevent our nation from running the course which has hitherto marked the destiny of nations. But, if I may even flatter myself that they may be productive of some partial benefit, some occasional good; that they may now and then recur to moderate the fury of party spirit, to warn against the mischiefs of foreign intrigue, to guard against the impostures of pretended patriotism; this hope will be a full recompense for the solicitude for your welfare, by which they have been dictated.

"How far in the discharge of my official duties I have been guided by the principles which have been delineated, the public records and other evidences of my conduct must witness to you and to the world. To myself, the assurance of my own conscience is, that I have at least believed myself to be guided by them[...]

"Though, in reviewing the incidents of my administration, I am unconscious of intentional error, I am nevertheless too sensible of my defects not to think it probable that I may have committed many errors. Whatever they may be, I fervently beseech the Almighty to avert or mitigate the evils to which they may tend. I shall also carry with me the hope that my country will never cease to view them with indulgence; and that, after forty five years of my life dedicated to its service with an upright zeal, the faults of incompetent abilities will be consigned to oblivion, as myself must soon be to the mansions of rest.

"Relying on its kindness in this as in other things, and actuated by that fervent love towards it, which is so natural to a man who views in it the native soil of himself and his progenitors for several generations, I anticipate with pleasing expectation that retreat in which I promise myself to realize, without alloy, the sweet enjoyment of partaking, in the midst of my fellow-citizens, the benign influence of good laws under a free government, the ever-favorite object of my heart, and the happy reward, as I trust, of our mutual cares, labors, and dangers."

--from George Washington's Farewell Address, delivered at the end of his second term of office, 1796.

Two

John Adams

(1735-1826)

Time in Office

1797-1801

John Adams was born in Braintree, Massachusetts on October 30, 1735, the oldest son of John Adams Sr., a farmer, and his wife, Susanna Boylston. Adams was descended from Puritans who had emigrated to New England in the early 17th century. As a boy, he was educated at a local "Dame school", and later attended Braintree Latin School, where he studied Latin, mathematics, and philosophy. As a teenager, he studied at Harvard College and embarked on an early career as a teacher. Dissatisfied with his prospects, Adams began studying the law, and in 1758, at the age of twenty-three, he was admitted to the bar. In 1764, Adams married Abigail Smith, a distant cousin. The couple would have six children, three boys and two girls, though two of their daughters died in infancy. Their oldest son, John Quincy Adams, would become the sixth president of the United States.

Escalating tensions between the colonial government and British rule during the 1760s influenced Adams to take an interest in politics and political theory. He wrote a number of pseudonymous essays criticizing British taxation measures, and became famous in Boston for his vocal opposition to the Stamp Act in 1765. He was selected by the state legislator to deliver an address to the royal governor of Massachusetts championing the "natural rights" that American colonists deserved to enjoy as British subjects. After the events of the 1770 Boston Massacre, in which a regiment of British soldiers fired on an unarmed mob of American protestors, Adams defended the soldiers in court and succeeded in securing their acquittal.

Adams was elected as a delegate to the First and Second Continental Congress, where he was given responsibility for drafting official documents and correspondences. It was John Adams who first nominated George Washington of Virginia to head the newly formed Continental Army after the outbreak of hostilities with England. Adams spent much of the war in Europe, principally in France and the Netherlands, attempting to secure foreign aid for the revolutionary effort. At the war's end, he returned to the United States briefly before resuming his diplomatic career abroad. In 1785, Adams became the first American ambassador to England. Four years later, he was recalled to the United States, where he served as the first American vice-president, under George Washington.

Adams was dissatisfied by the limited powers of the office of the vice-presidency, but enjoyed presiding over the Senate. Adams, like most of the Founding Fathers who hailed from the northern colonies, was a Federalist, and used his influence to strengthen the centrality of state and federal governments. When George Washington announced in 1796 that he would not seek a third term as president, Adams stood for election against Thomas Jefferson, Thomas Pinckney, Aaron Burr, and others. He was elected as the second president of the United States with only a three-point lead over Thomas Jefferson, who became his vice-president. Other members of his cabinet included Timothy Pickering and John Marshall, who both served as secretary of state, Oliver Wolcott, the secretary of the treasury, James McHenry, secretary of war, attorney general Charles Lee, and Benjamin Stoddert, who was appointed to the new office of secretary of the navy. Adams would be the first American president to see the White House (then called the President's Mansion) after construction was finished in the newly established capital city of Washington.

The unity of purpose which had seemed to characterize Washington's first term in office had entirely eroded by the time Adams became president. Bitter partisan conflict had erupted between Federalists and Democratic-Republicans. Adams's presidency commenced under the threat of war with France, where the revolution had toppled the monarchy, leaving Americans uncertain whether they should continue to honor the mutual defense treaties established with the French during the reign of Louis XVI. One of the more notable features of Adams' time in office was his signing of the Alien and Sedition Acts, which aimed to silence critics of the Federalist establishment. The massive unpopularity of the Acts, and Adam's public feuds with Alexander Hamilton, were chiefly responsible for Adams's defeat in the next election. The Federalist party would never again elect another president.

Disillusioned by his losses, Adams left Washington at the end of his term of office and returned to his house, called Peacefield, in his home town of Braintree, where he returned to farming and writing, and began work on an autobiography which was never completed. Believing that conscientious citizens had a duty to support the president in office "as far as we can in justice", Adams chose not to publicly criticize his successor, Thomas Jefferson. Though Jefferson and Adams had been at odds with one another since 1801, they began corresponding with one another several years after the end of Jefferson's presidency, and exchanged over a hundred letters between 1812 and 1824.

John Adams lived to see his oldest son, John Quincy Adams, elected president. Sixteen months later, he died quietly at home at Peacefield, having survived his wife Abigail, all three of his daughters, and his second son, Charles. The date of his death was July 4, 1826, exactly fifty-six years after the signing of the Declaration of Independence. On his death bed, he comforted himself with the reflection that his friend and fellow Founding Father Thomas Jefferson still lived, not knowing that Jefferson himself had died a few hours earlier that very day.

Memorable quote:

"I pray Heaven to bestow the best of blessings on this house and all that shall hereafter inhabit it. May none but honest and wise men ever rule under this roof."

--from a letter to Abigail Adams, regarding the newly constructed White House. President Franklin D. Roosevelt would later have these words inscribed over the mantel of the White House's State Dining Room.

Three

Thomas Jefferson

(1743-1826)

Time in Office

(1801-1809)

Thomas Jefferson, third president of the United States, was born on April 13, 1743, at Shadwell, a Virginia plantation near the city of Charlottesville. His parents were Peter Jefferson, a wealthy farmer and surveyor, and Jane Randolph Jefferson, whose family was amongst the most prominent landowning families in Virginia.

Jefferson had six sisters and one younger brother who survived to adulthood. As a boy, he was educated at Shadwell by private tutors, and later attended a small boarding school run by a local minister. Curious and inclined to intellectual pursuits, he excelled in Latin, Greek, and French, and also studied science and history. In 1762, at the age of nineteen, he graduated after two years of study from the College of William and Mary in Williamsburg, Virginia, where he read widely and was exposed to the works of John Locke, Isaac Newton, and other British rationalists. He also cultivated his musical abilities, acquiring a proficiency at the violin. After graduating, he began to study the law, and was admitted to the bar in Virginia in 1767, after which he began his law practice.

Jefferson was a lifelong slave owner who believed in the racial inferiority of blacks, but he exemplified the contradictions of his class and era by pursuing limited slavery reform both as a lawyer and as a member of the Virginia House of Burgesses, arguing that slave owners had the right to emancipate their own slaves without first seeking the approval of the British government. He also represented seven cases brought by slaves suing their masters for their freedom.

Jefferson's tenure in the Virginia House of Burgesses, which overlapped with George Washington's, lasted from 1769 to 1775, during which time he established himself as an ardent opponent of the so-called Intolerable Acts, taxes which were levied against the colonists by the British Parliament in order to recoup losses from the French and Indian War. His pamphlet, "A Summary View of the Rights of British America", which decried the unprecedented degree of British interference in colonial government, was published in 1774.

Jefferson's father had died when Jefferson was fourteen, making him the heir to Shadwell, but by 1768 he had already begun construction on the estate now famously associated with his name, Monticello. By 1770 building was complete. In 1772, Jefferson married a twenty-four-year old widow named Martha Skelton, and the couple took up residence at Monticello, where they had five daughters and one son; only two of their daughters, Martha and Mary, lived to adulthood. Martha Jefferson died in 1782, at the age of 33, after a difficult childbirth. Jefferson was deeply affected by this loss, and honored the deathbed promise he made to Martha not to remarry, so as to spare their children from the unkind treatment of a stepmother who might resent them. Jefferson had a series of mistresses and dalliances throughout his life, though the woman he is most commonly associated with now was a slave named Sally Hemings, inherited by Jefferson after the death of his father-in-law, who was said to have been Martha Jefferson's half-sister. Hemings, who was more than thirty years younger than Jefferson, had six children, all or most of whom are believed to have been fathered by Jefferson.

Jefferson was selected as one of the Virginia delegates to the Second Continental Congress in 1775, where he was asked to compose a draft of the Declaration of Independence, in consultation with the other members of the Committee of

Five: John Adams, Benjamin Franklin, Roger Sherman, and Robert Livingston. In 1776, he returned to Virginia to serve in the newly-established House of Delegates, where he authored and advocated for the Virginia Statute of Religious Freedom, a forerunner to the religious freedom clause of the Constitutional Bill of Rights. Three years later, Jefferson was elected governor of Virginia, serving from 1779 to 1781. After the end of the Revolutionary War Jefferson served for one year in Congress, before replacing Benjamin Franklin as the American ambassador to France. He returned to the United States in 1789, when newly-elected president George Washington named him secretary of state.

Jefferson immediately found himself at loggerheads with other members of Washington's cabinet, most notably Alexander Hamilton, the secretary of the treasury, who had been Washington's battlefield adjutant during the war. Out of this rivalry developed the formation of the first American political parties, with Jefferson leading the Democratic-Republicans, who felt that the Federalist position favoring strong federal government threatened to lead the new nation back down the path to European-style monarchy. After Washington stepped down from office in 1796, Jefferson ran for the presidency, losing to John Adams by a narrow margin. Having secured the second-largest number of votes, Jefferson became vice-president. He was a vocal critic of John Adams' Federalist policies, publishing the Kentucky and Virginia Resolutions, which argued that the federal government should not claim any powers not explicitly assigned to it by the Constitution, and that individual states should have the right to nullify any federal laws it disapproved of.

In the election of 1800, Jefferson again ran for president. He received the same number of votes as Aaron Burr, but unexpected support from his longtime political enemy Alexander Hamilton influenced the House of Representatives to cast the tie-breaking vote in Jefferson's favor. Burr, accordingly, served as Jefferson's vice-president during his first term in office, though his career famously ended in scandal after Burr killed Hamilton in a duel. Jefferson was sworn into office on 1801, the first president to be inaugurated in the new capital of Washington.

During his first administration, Jefferson oversaw the Louisiana Purchase, which more than doubled the size of the United States, as the French government ceded all French colonial territories below the 49th parallel to American control. Jefferson commissioned the famous exploratory expedition of Meriwether Lewis and William Clark to chart the new territories. Jefferson ran for re-election in 1804 against leading Federalist Charles Pinckney, who had served in Washington's cabinet. Unlike the last two elections, where the margin of victory was exceptionally narrow, Jefferson won for the second time with 70 per cent of the popular vote. During his second administration, Jefferson was chiefly concerned with keeping the United States out of the Napoleonic Wars then ongoing between France and England. In response to British harassment of American merchant vessels, Jefferson briefly closed American ports to trade with Europe. His efforts postponed the outbreak of war but did not neutralize it. Jefferson chose to follow George Washington's example and not seek a third term as president, and the War of 1812 would take place during the administration of his successor, James Madison.

From the end of his presidency in 1808 until his death in 1826, Jefferson remained at Monticello, pursuing hobbies such as the violin, architecture, and botany. He helped to design the University of Virginia, which would begin admitting students a year after his death; due his influence, it was the first institution of higher learning in the United States which did not require professions of faith from its students. Plagued by debt and financial troubles during the final years of his life, Jefferson died on the afternoon of July

4, 1826, at the age of 83. His estate was broken up and sold at public auction to clear his debts.

Memorable quote:

"The equal rights of man, and the happiness of every individual, are now acknowledged to be the only legitimate objects of government. Modern times have the signal advantage, too, of having discovered the only device by which these rights can be secured, to wit: government by the people, acting not in person, but by representatives chosen by themselves, that is to say; by every man of ripe years and sane mind, who either contributes by his purse or person to the support of his country."

--from a letter written by Thomas Jefferson to Adamantios Koraes, on the subject of the Greek revolutionary cause, 1823.

Four

James Madison

(1751-1836)

Time in Office

(1809-1817)

James Madison was born to parents James
Madison Sr. and Nellie Conway on March 16,
1751, at their plantation, Belle Grove, near Port
Conway, Virginia. The eldest of twelve children,
Madison had seven brothers and four sisters,
though only six of his siblings lived to be adults,
and Madison himself was sickly throughout
childhood. Madison's childhood and upbringing
were similar to Thomas Jefferson's. As the son of
one of the wealthiest planters in the Piedmont,
he was educated along classical lines by a private
tutor in subjects such as mathematics,
geography, and languages. Though most of his

generation of wealthy Virginians pursued their university education at the College of William and Mary, Madison took up studies at the College of New Jersey (now known as Princeton University) in 1769, because the northern climate was thought to be healthier. At college, Madison was the founder of the American Whig Society, a debating club which championed the cause of American independence. Madison was a dedicated student, completing his studies at an accelerated pace and remaining at college an additional year to study Hebrew and political theory. He returned to Virginia in 1772, at the age of twenty-one.

Like Jefferson and Washington, Madison spent the years leading up to the American revolution involved in local politics. He served on the Orange County Committee of Safety, which oversaw the militia, and later attained a colonel's rank in the Orange County militia, though his weak health prevented him from ever seeing battle. He also served in the Virginia legislature, and was one of Thomas Jefferson's Councilors of State while Jefferson was serving as governor of Virginia during the Revolutionary War. The two men became close friends during this period, a bond which would sustain them throughout their political careers. Like Jefferson, Madison was accounted crucial to wartime leadership in Virginia.

Madison was one of the chief critics of the Articles of Confederation, the first version of the American constitution. His extensive reading in political theory and systematic study of forms of government worldwide impressed upon him the necessity of a strong federal government that possessed the ability to collect taxes, impose tariffs, and support a standing national army. Under the Articles of Confederation, power was concentrated in the governments of the individual states. Though Madison would eventually break with other Federalists, he was an early supporter of the federalist agenda, a proponent for national assumption of state debt, and the ability to regulate state governments. He also emphasized the need for checks and balances between the three branches of government.

At the 1787 Constitutional Convention, Madison, along with other supporters such as Edmund Randolph, proposed the Virginia Plan, a map for the new federal government, which delineated the responsibilities of the legislative, executive, and judicial branches of government. The Virginia plan also called for the establishment of an upper and lower house of the federal legislature, in which states with larger populations were entitled to a larger number of representatives than states with smaller populations. Since this arrangement disproportionately benefitted the more populous southern states, northern delegates proposed the alternative New Jersey Plan, which called for one legislative house in which each state was entitled to one representative with one vote apiece. The Connecticut Compromise, which informed the final version of the Constitution, united aspects of both the Virginia and New Jersey Plans. Two legislative houses were established, the Senate and the House of Representatives; the Senate contained one senator from each state, while representation in House was made proportional by state population. Due to Madison's critical role in designing the forms of American federal government, he is remembered today as "the Father of the Constitution", though Madison distanced himself from this epithet in life, asserting that the Constitution had been the work of many people.

Madison supported the Constitution during the long process of ratification. Together with Founding Fathers Alexander Hamilton and John Jay, Madison wrote a series of essays explaining and defending the principles of government laid out in the Constitution as it was written. Eighty-five essays, published pseudonymously under the title "The Federalist Papers", were produced in total, with Madison contributing over thirty of them. Thanks in large part to his efforts, the Constitution was ratified by Congress in 1787, and ratified by the states the following year.

With the Constitution in place, the work of government could begin. George Washington was unanimously elected president, and James Madison was elected to represent Virginia in the newly formed U.S. House of Representatives. As a member of Congress, Madison was instrumental in drawing up the Bill of Rights, the first ten amendments to the Constitution which spelled out protections for specific rights to which all Americans were entitled, such as freedom of speech, religion, assembly, and privacy. The Bill of Rights was at last ratified by the states in 1791, and Madison served in the House for another six years, until 1797. Once Congress had been established under the terms of the new Constitution, it became a far more powerful body, capable of collecting taxes from the states and imposing uniform federal law. As Congress became more powerful, however,

Madison and his colleagues, chiefly Thomas Jefferson, began to fear that the federal government had become too powerful, with too much potential to interfere in the affairs of the states and private citizens. At this point, Madison began to separate himself from the Federalists, particularly after secretary of the treasury Alexander Hamilton proposed his plan to establish a national bank which would have the power to assume the debts of the states and establish national credit overseas. In response, Madison, along with Thomas Jefferson and James Monroe, became the leaders of the nation's first opposition party, the Democratic-Republicans, who regarded Federalists as near-monarchists who sought to make the American president into a king-like figure. Their belief was that American liberty could best be preserved by making the states as autonomous as possible, a sentiment far more popular in the larger, more agrarian southern states than in the smaller, more densely populated northern states.

In 1794, at the age of forty-three, Madison married Dolley Payne Todd, a Quaker widow of 26, who had one son by her previous marriage. Dolley Madison would go on to become the first truly legendary First Lady in American history, the first woman to preside over the White House and gain a reputation as a celebrated political hostess.

James Madison was appointed secretary of state in 1801 by Thomas Jefferson, and he would remain in that office until the end of Jefferson's second term as president. As secretary of state, Madison was chiefly responsible for overseeing the purchase of the Louisiana Territory in 1803. Madison. As the prospect of war with France or England loomed during the Napoleonic Wars of the early nineteenth century, Madison endeavored to keep the United States neutral, but established an embargo on foreign trade as retribution for British harassment of American ships. Though the embargo ended with Jefferson's presidency, war was still to come.

James Madison was elected the fourth president of the United States in 1808, defeating Charles Cotesworth Pinckney, a Federalist. Hostilities between England and the United States escalated during Madison's first term, as British ships progressed from harassing American sailors to kidnapping them and forcing them into the service of the British navy, and as the British allied with various Native American tribes against American settlers. Madison declared war in 1812, shortly before he was to run for re-election. However, the American army was nowhere near the same strength it had been during the Revolution. Congress regarded the war as Madison's personal vendetta, referring to it as "Mr. Madison's War", and the state militias were unwilling to supply troops until the British began to attack in earnest. Though American military forces on land were disorganized and met with frequent defeats, the sturdiness of American ships made them formidable opponents at sea. Madison was elected to a second term in office, this time defeating DeWitt Clinton, an anti-war candidate and a Federalist who nonetheless had the support of many Democratic-Republicans who opposed the war. Madison's popularity plummeted as wartime embargoes against overseas trade damaged the American economy, leading to threats of secession from the northern states.

The War of 1812 reached its crisis in 1814, when the British invaded Washington. James and Dolley Madison were forced to flee the White House, Dolley Madison remaining behind to oversee the removal and safekeeping of important American historical artifacts, such as copies of original state documents like the Declaration of Independence and the Constitution, as well as portraits of George Washington and other Founding Fathers. In the end, the White House, the Capitol, and the Library of Congress were invaded and burned by British soldiers. The War of 1812 came to a negotiated end after the signing of the Treaty of Ghent in December 1814, after which Madison's reputation recovered significantly.

Madison completed his second term in office in 1817, whereupon he retired with his wife to Montpelier, which was located near Thomas Jefferson's home of Monticello. Like Jefferson, and George Washington, who were also plantation owners, his personal finances had suffered considerably from neglecting his personal affairs during the years he was active in government. Like Jefferson, Madison maintained a policy of keeping to himself any critical views he might have held regarding his successors to the presidency, though he made himself available to give counsel to presidents such as Andrew Jackson when requested. In later years, Madison, who was one of the most prominent slaveholders among the Founding Fathers, became critical of the increasing strength of the abolitionist movement in the northern states. Madison worked alongside

Thomas Jefferson to design the University of Virginia, and in 1826 he became its rector. James Madison died at Montpelier on June 28, 1836, at the age of eighty-five.

Memorable quote:

"Wherever the real power in a Government lies, there is the danger of oppression. In our Governments, the real power lies in the majority of the Community, and the invasion of private rights is chiefly to be apprehended, not from the acts of Government contrary to the sense of its constituents, but from acts in which the Government is the mere instrument of the major number of the constituents."

--James Madison, from a 1788 letter to Thomas Jefferson.

Five

James Monroe

(1758-1831)

Time in Office

(1817-1825)

James Monroe was born April 28, 1758 in Westmoreland County, Virginia, to Spence Monroe, a moderately prosperous farmer and carpenter, and his wife, Elizabeth Jones. Spence Monroe's Scottish forebears had settled in the New World in the 1600s, but Elizabeth Jones's father was a wealthy recent Welsh immigrant to America. Monroe had one older sister, Elizabeth, and three younger brothers, Spence, Andrew, and Joseph.

Compared to his near neighbors Thomas Jefferson and James Madison, Monroe led a slightly less privileged life during his early childhood. He was enrolled in school at the age of eleven, but he was only able to attend for three months a year, since he was expected to help run the family farm. His father died when Monroe was sixteen, Monroe had to leave school entirely to look after his younger siblings. In 1774, however, he became a student at the College of William and Mary in Williamsburg, Virginia, where he was swiftly drawn into the cause of American independence.

While at William and Mary, the teenage Madison joined a group of fellow students who stole 200 muskets and 300 swords from the arsenal of the royal governor of Virginia, which they gave in turn to the local colonial militia. In 1776, at the age of eighteen, James Monroe was commissioned an officer in the new Continental Army. He fought as part of George Washington's forces during the ill-fated battle against the English for control of New York. During the Battle of Trenton, Monroe was severely wounded, and was promoted to the rank of captain by George Washington in recognition of his valor. Since American soldiers were badly provisioned, officers who could afford to do frequently paid for their men's clothing, weapons, and even their food, out of their own pocket. Since Monroe was not wealthy enough to do this, he asked to be transferred to Washington's general staff, where he became close friend the French noble the Marquis de Lafayette, who was fighting on the American side.

Alongside Washington and his officers, Monroe suffered the bitter cold and privation that characterized the 1777 winter encampment at Valley Forge. In 1779, Monroe resigned his commission under Washington and entered the Virginia militia as a colonel. During this phase of the war, the British were focusing their main strength against the southern colonies, so Thomas Jefferson, then governor of Virginia, tasked Monroe with traveling to North Carolina to scout British troop movements. Monroe would be the last American president who had served as an officer during the Revolutionary War, which is why the end of his second term is considered the end of the Revolutionary era in American politics.

After the war's conclusion, Monroe read law under Thomas Jefferson's supervision, and at the same time was elected to the Continental Congress of 1783. While in New York, then the seat of Congress, Monroe became acquainted with Elizabeth Kortright, whose father was a founding member of the New York Chamber of Commerce. They were married on February 16, 1786; Elizabeth was seventeen and Monroe twenty-seven. The couple would go on to have three children: Eliza, James, and Maria. After Congress was adjourned, Monroe and his young family returned to Virginia, settling in Fredericksburg, where Monroe practiced law.

The year after his marriage, Monroe was elected to the Virginia assembly, and in 1788, he was appointed as a delegate to the Virginia Ratifying

Convention. He had been unable to attend the Constitutional Congress due to the demands of his law practice. Monroe was among a large number of delegates who opposed ratification on the grounds that the Constitution did not provide adequately for the individual liberties of citizens; these concerns were later addressed in the first amendments to the Constitution, known as the Bill of Rights. In 1790, Monroe ran unsuccessfully against James Madison for a seat in the First Congress of the United States. Despite his narrow defeat, he was appointed to Congress by the Virginia state legislature later that year to finish out the term of Senator William Grayson, who had died unexpectedly. Madison, as a member of Congress, quickly aligned himself with the anti-Federalist coalition of Thomas Jefferson and James Madison's Democratic-Republican party. George Washington appointed Monroe as the American ambassador to France in 1794. In France, Monroe's pro-republican sentiments won acclaim, and he was able to use his influence to persuade the revolutionary government of France to release certain political prisoners, such as philosopher Thomas Paine, and Adrienne de Lafayette, the wife of the Marquis de Lafayette. At the insistence of prominent Federalists, Washington recalled Monroe to the United States in 1797.

From 1799 to 1802, Monroe served as governor of Virginia, elected to three one-year terms. Then, in 1803, President Thomas Jefferson dispatched Monroe to France again, this time to personally oversee negotiations for the sale of the Louisiana Territory. Afterwards, Monroe's diplomatic career continued apace: he was the American ambassador to England for four years between 1803 and 1807, and during that same period he served briefly as a special envoy to Spain. When Monroe returned to the United States again, he was persuaded by other members of the Democratic-Republican party to run against James Madison in the 1808 presidential election, though he correctly foresaw that he would have little chance of victory against Madison. After serving another term as governor of Virginia, he was named secretary of state by James Madison, and later secretary of war. When Madison chose to follow George Washington's example and not seek a third term as president, Monroe decided to run in earnest, and won an overwhelming victory again Federalist Rufus King, winning sixteen out of nineteen states. Monroe emulated George Washington as president by commencing his administration with a fifteen-week presidential tour through the northern states, which made him the most recognizable president of the era.

It is due to Monroe that the last years of the early republic were known as "the Era of Good Feelings". The War of 1812 had been brought to a satisfactory conclusion, the American economy was recovering, and Monroe himself had a talent for projecting affability and accessibility which won the confidence of the people. Later in his administration, however, the lingering amity and unity of purpose which had guided the American government during the post-revolutionary period began to disintegrate, as tensions escalated over the balance of power between slave states and free states. In 1819, Missouri sought entry to the Union as a slave state, provoking protests from northern abolitionists as well as from whites in the west who resented having to compete with slave labor. The more slave states there were, the more slavery expansionists there would be in Congress, threatening the power of the free states. The temporary solution agreed upon was the Missouri Compromise: for every slave state admitted to the Union, a free state would also have to be admitted. Missouri therefore entered the United States as a slave state, while the northernmost counties of Massachusetts were allowed to secede and reorganize as the free state of Maine. The Compromise also established the so-called Mason-Dixon line. North of the line, in the new territories encompassed by the Louisiana Purchase, slavery would be prohibited.

Though the Federalist platform had not vanished from American government, the Federalist party was no longer a force to be reckoned with, and during Monroe's first term it seemed as if the United States had returned to the nonpartisan spirit of George Washington's administration. But during Monroe's second term, new party line began to be drawn along pro and anti slavery lines. The tension over slavery would define American politics for the next four decades, until the Civil War. The era of Federalists versus Democratic-Republicans was over; the era of Democrats versus Whigs had begun.

The most enduring legacy of James Monroe's presidency is the Monroe Doctrine. The United States had made repeated overtures to the government of Spain regarding its colonial possessions in Florida, but Spain had refused to sell Florida to the Americans. Then, in 1818, Monroe sent General Andrew Jackson to Florida, ostensibly to suppress Seminole raids carried out against white settlers. Jackson seized the opportunity to press southward and seize two Spanish forts, an exercise which proved to the Spanish that they did not have the resources to maintain their hold over Florida while their colonies in Central America were in revolt. Monroe's secretary of state, John Quincy Adams, was able to negotiate the sale of Florida to the United States shortly afterward. When the former Spanish colonies of Argentina, Chile, Colombia, Mexico, and Peru fought successful revolutions against Spanish imperialism, Monroe delivered a message to Congress in December of 1823 declaring that European colonialism in the Western Hemisphere was to be opposed, that the government of the United States would support all new republican governments and help defend them from any attempt by European powers to regain possession of their colonies. The New World was now closed to new European colonization. The

Monroe Doctrine has been one of the guiding lights of American foreign policy ever since.

After leaving office at the end of his second term, Monroe and his wife return to Virginia, where they owned an estate in Loudoun County. Like all of his presidential predecessors, Monroe suffered serious financial losses during his years in government service, and was forced to apply to the government for help recovering them. Monroe lived in Virginia until the death of his wife Elizabeth in 1830. Afterwards, he moved to his daughter's home in New York, where he died on July 4, 1831.

Memorable quote:

"...At the proposal of the Russian Imperial Government, made through the minister of the Emperor residing here, a full power and instructions have been transmitted to the minister of the United States at St. Petersburg to arrange by amicable negotiation the respective rights and interests of the two nations on the northwest coast of this continent. A similar proposal has been made by His Imperial Majesty to the Government of Great Britain, which has likewise been acceded to. The Government of the United States has been desirous by this friendly proceeding of manifesting the great value which they have invariably attached to the friendship of the Emperor and their solicitude to cultivate the best understanding with his Government. In the discussions to which this interest has given rise and in the arrangements by which they may terminate the occasion has been judged proper for asserting, as a principle in which the rights and interests of the United States are involved, that the American continents, by the free and independent condition which they have assumed and maintain, are henceforth not to be considered as subjects for future colonization by any European powers..."

--excerpt from the Monroe Doctrine, 1823.

Part Two: The Transcendental Awakening

Six

John Quincy Adams

(1767-1848)

Time in Office

(1825-1829)

John Quincy Adams, the eldest son of John Adams, was the first American president to be preceded in that office by a family member. He was born in Braintree, Massachusetts on July 11, 1767, to John and Abigail Adams, the oldest of their four surviving children. Adams's life was dominated by his father's role in American politics from a very early age, and his education reflected this fact, as the elder Adams groomed him for a life of public service to the new nation.

In 1775, at the age of eight, John Quincy Adams witnessed the Battle of Bunker Hill from the vantage point of his family's farm in Braintree. By the age of ten, he was accompanying John Adams on his diplomatic travels to France and the Netherlands. When Adams was recalled to the United States, he sent 14 year-old Quincy to Russia as a secretary and translator to the American envoy Francis Dana, who was tasked with gaining Russian support for the Revolution. Two years later, he served as his father's secretary during negotiations for the Treaty of Paris. His education was wide-ranging but eccentric, as he studied under the tutelage of his father's law clerks and attended a variety of schools and universities in Europe, before returning the United States in 1785 and completing a degree at Harvard University two years later.

John Quincy Adams began his law practice in Boston in 1790, but in 1793 he was appointed by President George Washington to serve as the

American ambassador to the Netherlands. Four years later, after John Adams became president, he was appointed ambassador to Prussia (part of present-day Germany.) In 1797, while fulfilling his diplomatic functions in Europe, he married Louisa Johnson, daughter of first U.S. consul to Britain. His time in Prussia came to an end, however, after John Adams lost his bid for re-election. In 1802 Adams was elected to the state legislature in Massachusetts, and the following year he was elected to the U.S. Senate. Adams's personal politics reflected the rapidly changing political climate of the early Republic. Though nominally a Federalist like his father, and supporting much of the Federalist platform, he found it comparatively easy to establish common ground with Democratic-Republicans, which enabled him to function as a member of Thomas Jefferson's cabinet. After James Madison was elected president, Adams resigned from the Senate and formally switched his party allegiance to the Democratic-Republicans, though it would not be the last party switch of his career.

In 1809, Adams returned to Russia, this time as President James Madison's ambassador to Russia. Five years later he was recalled in order to oversee negotiations during the Treaty of Ghent, which brought an end to the hostilities of the War of 1812. In 1813, Adams resumed his diplomatic functions and became the American ambassador to Britain, a post first held by his father. Adams's most influential role prior to his presidency was as secretary of state under James Monroe, in which capacity he secured the purchase of Florida by the United States from Spain and negotiated the disputed border between British and American holdings in the Oregon territory.

Adams was thirty by the time his father became president, and he was in his late fifties when he himself was elected in 1824. Adams was one of five Democratic-Republican candidates on the ballot during the 1824 election, and when the first vote produced no clear victor, Kentucky statesman Henry Clay dropped out of the race and gave his support to Adams, ensuring his decisive victory. Adams' election of 1824 was the first election in which a candidate lost the popular vote but won the electoral college. Andrew Jackson, one of Adams's opponents, was incensed by the outcome of the vote, and alleged corruption and impropriety against Adams after he appointed Henry Clay his secretary of state.

Historians regard Adams' four years as president as among the least important of his achievements over a lifelong career in public service. As president, the irascible temper he inherited from his father made it difficult for him to form and maintain political alliances, and by the end of his one term in office he had alienated key members of his own party. Adams's domestic policy proposals, which encompassed an interconnected network of roads and canals spanning across the United States, would be championed by future presidents such as

Abraham Lincoln, who understood the necessity of connecting far-flung frontier settlements to more populated areas, but in Adams's time such proposals were considered overly ambitious and beyond the young nation's resources. Adams was accused of attempting to expand the powers of the federal government and diminish the autonomy of state and local governments. By the time of the 1826 midterm elections, Adams's party had lost control of Congress, and his agenda was effectively stymied for the rest of his administration.

Adams ran for re-election in 1828, but did not win a second term in office. During this era, presidential candidates did not openly campaign on their own behalf, but rather allowed their supporters to drum up public support for them. A massive scandal erupted during the 1828 campaign after Adams's supporters exposed the fact that Rachel Jackson, the wife of Adams's opponent Andrew Jackson, had married him bigamously, in the mistaken belief that her first husband had divorced her prior to their nuptials. When she died a short time later, Jackson and his supporters accused Adams's camp of hounding her to her grave, and whatever popular support Adams had enjoyed before that point evaporated. He lost the election by a large margin, and chose to leave the capital before Jackson's inauguration took place.

Two years after the end of Adams's presidency, he won a seat in the House of Representatives, where he served for the next eighteen years. As a Congressman and statesman, his was one of the loudest and most respected voices against slavery during the slavery-expansionist years leading up to the Civil War. In 1836, Southerners attempted to impose a gag-rule on the slavery debate in Congress, which was defeated due largely to Adams's vehement opposition. In 1841, when kidnapped Africans being transported to the U.S. to be sold as slaves seized control of a ship called the *Amistad*, Adams represented them in court and won their acquittal and freedom.

John Quincy Adams had perhaps one of the most poignant deaths of any American president. On February 23, 1848, while giving an impassioned speech supporting the rights of veterans of the Mexican-American War, he suffered a massive cerebral hemorrhage. He was carried to a nearby room in the Capitol, where he died after two days.

Memorable quotes:

"There is one principle which pervades all the institutions of this country, and which must always operate as an obstacle to the granting of favors to new comers. This is a land, not of privileges, but of equal rights. Privileges are granted by European sovereigns to particular classes of individuals, for purposes of general policy; but the general impression here is that privileges granted to one denomination of people, can very seldom be discriminated from erosions of the rights of others. [Immigrants], coming here, are not to expect favors from the governments. They are to expect, if they choose to become citizens, equal rights with those of the natives of the country. They are to expect, if affluent, to possess the means of making their property productive, with moderation, and with safety;—if indigent, but industrious, honest and frugal, the means of obtaining easy and comfortable subsistence for themselves and their families. They come to a life of independence, but to a life of labor—and, if they cannot accommodate themselves to the character, moral, political, and physical, of this country, with all its compensating balances of good and evil, the Atlantic is always open to them, to return to the land of their nativity and their fathers."

--from a letter written by John Quincy Adams in 1819, while serving as James Monroe's secretary of state.

Seven

Andrew Jackson

(1767-1845)

Time in Office

(1829-1837)

On March 15, 1767, Andrew Jackson was born to a widow named Elizabeth Jackson; Jackson's father had died three weeks before his youngest son's birth. Recent immigrants from Ireland, the Jacksons, including the two older sons, Hugh and Robert, and other assorted relatives, had settled in Waxhaw, a territory which lies across the North Carolina-South Carolina border, just south of Charlotte. The area was considered wilderness terrain when Jackson was a boy, as it had not been thoroughly explored by white surveyors, so the exact location of Jackson's birth cannot now be traced.

Though James Monroe is considered to be the last American president to have fought in the Revolutionary War, the distinction might also be said to apply to Andrew Jackson, whose early childhood was entirely dominated by the war against the British. When the British began a campaign of total war in the American south, Jackson's mother encouraged Andrew and his brother Robert to train with the local militia for their own protection, though Andrew was barely a teenager at the time. His eldest brother, Hugh, who had enlisted in the American army, had already died of heat stroke in the midst of battle in 1779. In 1781, both Robert and Andrew Jackson were captured by the British. They were subjected to prisoner abuse during their captivity and contracted smallpox before their mother successfully bargained for their release. They were forced to make the long journey home mostly on foot in inclement weather, which worsened both boys' illness. Andrew's life was despaired of, and his brother died on April 27, 1781. Andrew Jackson eventually recovered, though he lost his mother later that year when she died of cholera, which she contracted while volunteering to nurse American prisoners of war. Jackson would cherish a bitter lifelong hatred against the British for the deaths of his brothers and mother.

When the Revolutionary War ended, Jackson was sent to Charleston, South Carolina, to complete his education. His war-torn childhood had not molded him into a quiet, well-behaved pupil, and he gained a reputation for having high spirits and a nearly ungovernable temper. When Jackson was seventeen, he became a teacher briefly before gaining his law license in 1787 and starting a legal practice in Salisbury, North Carolina. He also worked odd jobs as a shop clerk during this period. Later that year, judge John McNairy, a friend of Jackson's, appointed him as a public prosecutor for the Nashville region, and Jackson spent the next several years in Tennessee, practicing law on the American frontier.

In 1788, Jackson became romantically involved with Rachel Donelson Robards, daughter of the landlord of the boarding house where he resided. She was married at the time, though her husband, who is thought to have been abusive, had left her, declaring his intention to seek a divorce. Believing that the divorce had taken place, Rachel and Jackson eloped to Natchez to be married, only to discover in 1791 that the divorce had never been granted. When Rachel's first husband learned of her relationship with Jackson, he divorced her for bigamy; Rachel and Jackson obtained a legal marriage in 1794. Their marriage produced no children, but the couple adopted and cared for a number of parentless children, including Rachel's nephews and a Muscogee orphan named Lyncoya, whom Jackson hoped to send to West Point.

During Jackson's early political career, he was one of the most energetic forces behind the organization of the Tennessee territory and the campaign for its admission to the Union as a state. In 1796, Jackson was a delegate to the Tennessee Constitutional Convention, and after statehood was granted, he served both as Tennessee's first Congressional representative to Washington and, later, as one of its first U.S. Senators. Unable to support himself financially in Washington, Jackson returned to Tennessee in 1799, where he served as a circuit court judge, lawyer, and businessman. By this time, he owned some 15 slaves, who produced whiskey at Jackson's private distillery. Through the course of his life, he is thought to have owned as many as 300 slaves in total. By the turn of the 19th century Jackson had become well-traveled, making business trips to most major American cities. He speculated in land, which nearly led to his becoming bankrupt, and forced him to sell his plantation and distillery.

Jackson first became a household name during the War of 1812. Jackson had initially been refused a commission by President James Madison, due to his reputation for recklessness, and his known association with former vice-president Aaron Burr, who was accused of treasonous conspiracy with Mexico. After Jackson was commissioned as a major general, he was entrusted with the defense of New Orleans, backed by 1500 soldiers. After Jackson's company was abruptly dissolved while still on their way to Louisiana, leaving his soldiers without money or means to return to Tennessee, Jackson earned the undying loyalty of his men by leading their march home personally, traveling on foot so that wounded soldiers could make use of his horse. Later that year, Jackson and a company of soldiers from Fayetteville, Tennessee, fought a war against the Shawnee, whose leader, Tecumseh, had been given support by the British in order to defend Shawnee land from white aggression. Jackson defeated Tecumseh's forces at the Battle of Horseshoe Bend and forced the surviving Native Americans to sign treaties giving up half their land to white settlers. Finally, in 1815, with New Orleans under threat once again, Jackson was given a command

and orders to prevent British troops from landing on American soil off the Gulf of Mexico. By the time Jackson won his famous victory over the British during the Battle of New Orleans, peace talks were already underway between British and American leadership, but Jackson's dramatic victory—2000 British killed or wounded compared to only 70 American casualties—instantly made him famous. As of 2018, no foreign power has attempted an invasion on American soil since the Battle of New Orleans.

The second stage of Jackson's military career involved an aggressive campaign against the Creek and Seminole people of Florida, which was then a Spanish colony. In response to Seminole attacks against white settlers who were encroaching on Native territory, Jackson exceeded his orders and forced the Seminoles south, capturing the city of Pensacola from the Spanish along the way. Because the capture of Pensacola led to Spain's agreeing to sell Florida to the United States, President James Monroe chose not to discipline him for breach of military orders and instead appointed him Florida's first American governor. Jackson's governorship lasted only six months, from July to December of 1821.

On the strength of his popularity after the War of 1812, Jackson once more obtained a Senate seat in 1822. His supporters nominated him to run in the presidential election of 1824, and though he lost to John Quincy Adams, he was well-positioned to run against Adams a second time in 1828. His wife, Rachel, died shortly after Jackson's election, and Jackson blamed his political enemies for her fatal heart attack, believing it to be the result of vicious attacks on her character published in the press by his political enemies. Rachel Jackson's niece, Emily Donelson, performed the official functions of First Lady during Jackson's presidency.

Andrew Jackson is today associated with the advent of "Jacksonian Democracy", the concept that the president serves as the voice and representative of the people, rather than as an appointed superior set over the nation to safeguard its best interest in the traditional, monarchial fashion. His politics were Jeffersonian in nature, focused on safeguarding America's agrarian society, which by its nature required support for the expansion of slavery. Jackson believed that the elite, or upper classes of American society, had been dominating politics to the detriment of the poor, and that even the least educated Americans were capable of making correct and informed political decisions.

Scandal had plagued Jackson's candidacy and scandal continued to plague him during his presidency. The Eaton Affair, also called the "Petticoat Affair", saw Jackson's dismissal of all but one member of his cabinet, after the wives of Jackson's other cabinet officials began to socially ostracize secretary of war John Eaton over rumors that he and his wife Peggy had been intimate prior to Peggy's divorce from her alcoholic first husband. By 1831, the only member of Jackson's cabinet still in office was the postmaster-general. Jackson began to rely heavily on the advice of trusted but unofficial advisors who were referred to pejoratively as Jackson's "Kitchen Cabinet"—implying that they were untrustworthy sorts who had to be received in the kitchen as they could not be seen in the front parlor. It is probably safe to say that Jackson redefined the role of the presidency more than any president before him save for George Washington. Where previous presidents had chosen not to exercise their rights of veto unless they believed that a bill was unconstitutional, Jackson vetoed any bill that was not, in his opinion, serving the best interests of the country. He attacked corruption in Washington and dismissed officials for incompetence as well as for supporting his political opponents. In 1832, Jackson accomplished the dearest wish of all anti-Federalists since the Revolution by refusing to renew the charter of the Second Bank of the United States, the precursor to the Treasury Department. Under Jackson's direction, America paid off its national debt for the first and only time in its history, but the lack of government spending led directly to the Panic of 1837 and a widespread depression.

In 1832, twenty-eight years before the start of the Civil War, South Carolina threatened to secede from the Union when federal protective tariffs threatened the state economy. South Carolina and other state's rights advocates believed that the individual states had the right under the Constitution to "nullify", that is, set aside and ignore, any federal legislation that ran counter to the interests of the states. Following his re-election in 1832, Jackson introduced legislation which would permit him to force South Carolina's compliance with the law via military force, but a compromise was reached before the secession crisis came to a head. Civil war had been narrowly averted, though threats of southern secession would dominate American politics for the next three decades.

In later eras, Jackson's legacy would be tainted by the Indian Removal Act of 1830, as a result of which thousands of Native Americans were forced out of their ancestral lands to make room for white settlers in the Western Expansion. While white settlers claimed the fertile land in the south for their own farms, Native Americans were removed at a forced march, during which thousands died, to reservations in Oklahoma and other parts of the Midwest.

In January of 1835, Andrew Jackson became the first American president to survive an assassination attempt, after an English immigrant fired two pistols at him in heavy rain, causing them both to misfire. Jackson responded to the assault by attacking his assailant with his cane.

In 1837, Jackson retired after his second term in office, and returned to his farm outside Nashville, called The Hermitage, where he kept some 150 slaves. Though he never again ran for or held public office, he continued to use his influence in matters that interested him, such as Texas' joining the Union in 1845. He was succeeded as president by his hand-picked replacement, vice-president Martin Van Buren, and assisted in the election of James K. Polk in 1844. That same year, he was obligated to retire from public life, as his health began to deteriorate. On June 8, 1845, he died at The Hermitage, at the age of 78. He was buried on the grounds of the estate.

Memorable quote:

"The bank, Mr. Van Buren, is trying to kill me, *but I will kill it.*"

--Andrew Jackson, in conversation to Martin Van Buren, as reported in Van Buren's memoirs.

Eight

Martin Van Buren

(1782-1862)

Time in Office

(1837-1841)

Martin Van Buren was born on December 5,
1782, in Kinderhook, New York, near Albany, to
Abraham and Maria Van Buren, who were
descended from the 17th century Dutch settlers of
the New York region. The couple had three
children from Maria's first marriage, and had
five children of their own, of whom Martin was
the third. Van Buren grew up speaking Dutch as
a boy, and was the first American president not
born of British ancestry. Though the Van Burens
were not wealthy, Abraham Van Buren earned a
comfortable living running a tavern, where
community political meetings often took place.

He was also a member of the Albany Militia during the Revolutionary War and a proponent of Jeffersonian democracy.

As a boy, Van Buren was educated in local schools, as well as the Kinderhook Academy, where he learned Latin, and at Washington Seminary. His formal education ended at the age of 14, due to his family's lack of funds. Van Buren began to study law under Peter and Francis Silvester, a father-and-son firm of Federalist attorneys. By 1803, when he was twenty-one, Van Buren had started his own law practice. He was married four years later to Hannah Hoes, his second cousin and close companion since childhood. Of their five children, all sons, four lived to adulthood. Van Buren's eldest son Abraham graduated from West Point and had a long military career; John, the second eldest, became Attorney General of New York; Martin Jr. served as his father's secretary until his death from tuberculosis; his youngest son, Smith, became a special advisor to Van Buren during his father's presidency.

Van Buren's political career began around the time of his marriage, as he grew more closely involved with the local branch of the Democratic-Republican party. He was elected to the state legislature of New York in 1812, and after three years was appointed Attorney General for New York. He proved to have a talent for forming and securing cooperative alliances with other prominent politicians, particularly those with wealthy connections who could be of financial use to him during future campaigns. He is considered to be the first major American politician to practice big donor politics.

Hannah Van Buren died of tuberculosis near the end of Van Buren's second term in the New York senate. He never remarried, raising his four sons as a single father while continuing to pursue his political career. In 1821, Van Buren was elected to the Senate. After John Quincy Adams's election in 1824, Van Buren became a founding member of the newly-minted Democratic Party, formed from the dregs of the Revolutionary-era Democratic-Republican party. Van Buren left the Senate in 1828 after his election as governor of New York, but he resigned the governorship only a few months later, after newly-elected president Andrew Jackson, on whose behalf Van Buren had campaigned, appointed him as his secretary of state. At Jackson's request, Van Buren resigned from office during the so-called "Kitchen Cabinet" scandal, and Jackson appointed Van Buren the American ambassador to Britain in exchange for this sacrifice.

In 1832, Van Buren was chosen as Andrew Jackson's running mate during the first Democratic National Convention, and when Jackson's second term came to an end in 1835, Van Buren ran for president at Jackson's urging, with the unanimous support of his party. He was elected president in 1836 with a clear majority over his Whig opponents, but his administration was immediately confronted with significant challenges, chiefly those stemming from the Panic of 1837, sparked by Jackson's closing of the Bank of the United States. Van Buren essentially inherited the worst financial crisis in American history to that point, as banks across the country failed and small business owners lost their livelihoods. Van Buren's proposed solution was to establish an independent national treasury for all federal funds, and though this measure would be adopted in time, it was not brought to fruition during Van Buren's administration.

Van Buren's early popularity disintegrated quickly, as the American public blamed him both for the financial crisis he had inherited from Jackson, and for his foreign policy stance towards Great Britain during a series of border skirmishes along the border between Maine and New Brunswick. Eager to avoid another war with Britain, Van Buren successfully negotiated a peaceful settlement, but this did not satisfy many Americans, who saw the negotiations as a missed opportunity to declare America's strength against its rivals. Van Buren also found himself on the losing side of the debate over whether to admit Texas to the Union. Additionally, Van Buren perpetuated Jacksonian-era genocidal policy towards Native Americans in the western frontier, policies which the American public had begun to decry as cruel and inhumane. When Van Buren ran for re-election in 1840, he again received the unanimous support of his party, but his reputation had suffered too great a decline—his detractors had taken to referring to him as "Martin Van Ruin". He was defeated by William Henry Harrison by a wide margin, failing even to secure the electoral votes from his home state of New York.

In 1841, Van Buren returned to Lindenwald, his Kinderhook estate. Despite his defeated re-election bid, he entertained hopes that he would receive the Democratic nomination for the 1844 election, only to lose the nomination to James Polk, a supporter of Texas annexation. Four years after Polk's election, in 1848, Van Buren ran for president a third time, as a member of the newly organized Free Soil Party, which opposed the expansion of slavery on the grounds that it forced white workers to compete for work against hired slave labor. He received only ten per cent of the vote, and did not attempt another presidential bid. For the next decade and a half, until his death in 1862, he traveled extensively and wrote a memoir of his political career. In 1861, Van Buren contracted tuberculosis, and after being bedridden for nearly a year, died at Lindenwald on July 24, 1862, where he was buried in a family plot.

Memorable quote:

"In receiving from the people the sacred trust twice confided to my illustrious predecessor, and which he has discharged so faithfully and so well, I know that I can not expect to perform the arduous task with equal ability and success. But united as I have been in his counsels, a daily witness of his exclusive and unsurpassed devotion to his country's welfare, agreeing with him in sentiments which his countrymen have warmly supported, and permitted to partake largely of his confidence, I may hope that somewhat of the same cheering approbation will be found to attend upon my path. For him I but express with my own the wishes of all, that he may yet long live to enjoy the brilliant evening of his well-spent life; and for myself, conscious of but one desire, faithfully to serve my country, I throw myself without fear on its justice and its kindness. Beyond that I only look to the gracious protection of the Divine Being whose strengthening support I humbly solicit, and whom I fervently pray to look down upon us all. May it be among the dispensations of His providence to bless our beloved country with honors and with length of days. May her ways be ways of pleasantness and all her paths be peace!"

--Martin Van Buren, from his inaugural address, 1837.

Part Three: Era of Slavery Expansion

Nine

William Henry Harrison

(1773-1841)

Time in Office

(March 4, 1841-April 4, 1841)

Descended from British settlers who arrived in Virginia in the early 1600s, William Henry Harrison was born February 9, 1773, at his family's Virginia plantation, called Berkeley, near present-day Richmond. Harrison's father, Benjamin Harrison V, was a founding father and signatory to the Declaration of Independence, as well as governor of Virginia for a time. Harrison was the seventh and youngest of the children of Benjamin and Elizabeth Basset Harrison, and he was the last American president to have been born a British subject under colonial rule. As a boy, Harrison was educated at home by private tutors, and at the age of fourteen he was enrolled at Hampden-Sydney College in Virginia. There, he studied for three years, reading the standard classical curriculum of Greek and Latin. Harrison's father eventually removed him from Hampden-Sydney, possibly because it was a Presbyterian institution and the Harrison family were Episcopalian. Harrison was sent to a boy's academy in Southampton briefly before enrolling in the University of Pennsylvania to study medicine. In 1791, at the age of eighteen, Harrison discontinued his academic studies in order to join the army.

After receiving his commission as an ensign, Harrison was assigned to Fort Washington, near present-day Cincinnati, in what was then known as the Northwest Territory (an area encompassing all territory west of Pennsylvania, east of the Mississippi, and northwest of the

Ohio River.) For the next several years, Harrison was embroiled in the Northwest Indian Wars against the Native American inhabitants of the western frontier. He was promoted to lieutenant in 1792 and served as aide-de-camp to Major General Anthony Wayne, fighting alongside him during the Battle of Fallen Timbers, which ended the war. He was promoted to captain after the battle. During this period, Harrison's mother died, leaving him heir to a substantial portion of the family estate, including 3000 acres of land and several slaves. Harrison sold the land to his brother, as he had no immediate plans to abandon his military career to be a farmer.

Harrison was married in 1795 to Anna Tuthill Symmes, the daughter of a prominent Ohio judge and land owner. The couple was forced to elope after Symmes's father forbade the match on the grounds that Harrison's career prospects in the army were not promising. The marriage produced ten children; all but one of their children survived to adulthood, though only four would still be living by the time Harrison was elected as president. His sixth son would become the father of the 23rd American president, Benjamin Harrison, making William Henry Harrison the only president to date who was succeeded by a grandchild, and the second American president to be followed in office by a family member.

In 1798, Harrison resigned from the army, and was promptly named secretary of the Northwest Territory by President John Adams; a year later, Harrison became the region's first delegate to Congress. A year after that, in 1800, the Northwest Territory was divided into smaller portions, one of which was the Indiana Territory, of which Harrison was named governor. Harrison's chief responsibility was to negotiate with the Native American peoples of the region on behalf of white settlers. Though he succeeded in establishing mutual treaties with several Indian nations which gave settlers access to millions of acres of frontier territory, Harrison used military force to drive out the indigenous peoples who refused to sign the treaties. In 1811, Harrison and U.S. forces fought the Shawnee nation at the famous Battle of Tippecanoe in Indiana. When Harrison ran for president twenty-nine years later, he invoked the popularity of this victory with the campaign slogan "Tippecanoe and Tyler too" (referring to his running mate, John Tyler.)

Harrison served as governor of the Indiana Territory for over a decade until the outbreak of the War of 1812, when he re-entered the army with the rank of brigadier general. He was appointed head of the Army of the Northwest, where his principle task was to fight the Native Americans who were being armed and supplied by the British to wreak havoc along the western front. He led American soldiers in the Battle of the Thames, fought in Ontario, Canada, against a unified band of Native American tribes led by Tecumseh. After Tecumseh's death, the indigenous armies were defeated and scattered.

After the war ended in 1814, Harrison retired from the army at the rank of major general and settled with his family in Ohio. In 1816, he was elected as an Ohio congressional representative, and served in that capacity for twelve years until he was appointed the U.S. ambassador to Colombia by President John Quincy Adams. He was recalled after only a year, when Adams was succeeded by the newly elected Andrew Jackson. Harrison's time in Bogota influenced him deeply, and he observed with concern the growing power of Simon Bolivar, fearing that he was likely to become a military dictator.

For the next two decades, William Henry Harrison lived a private life in retirement at his farm in North Bend, Ohio, living on the modest income provided by his military pension and his farm. Regarded as a national hero for his critical role in the second most important victory of the War of 1812, a number of biographies were written about him during this period, and Harrison gained a small income from the royalties from the books he agreed to be interviewed for. Though he operated a small corn distillery for a time, he became a teetotaler, and began regarding the production of liquor as sinful. In the 1830s, he also met and befriended a free man of color named George DeBaptiste, who worked secretly as a conductor on the Underground Railroad. Harrison eventually hired DeBaptiste as his personal servant, and the two remained together for the rest of Harrison's life.

In 1836, Harrison ran as a presidential candidate for the Whig Party against Martin Van Buren, and was soundly defeated. Re-nominated in 1840, with John Tyler as his running mate, Harrison faced criticism in the press on the grounds that, at the age of 68, he was more fit for retirement than for the office of the presidency. One newspaper article claimed that he would be better off with a pension and a log cabin where he could live out the rest of his days in peace. The Whig party seized upon this image, and

Harrison's presidential campaign became known as the "log cabin campaign", reinforcing Harrison's image as a humble man of the people, a political narrative which later presidents such as Abraham Lincoln would capitalize upon to great effect. Ironically, Harrison's opponent, Martin Van Buren, came from a genuinely humble background, whereas Harrison was raised amongst old landowning Virginia aristocracy. Harrison won a decisive victory in the electoral college and the popular vote.

William Henry Harrison was inaugurated as the ninth president of the United States on March 4, 1841, the oldest person ever to hold the office until the election of President Ronald Reagan in 1980. He also holds the record for the longest inaugural address ever delivered by a president, and the record for shortest term in presidential office. After delivering his inaugural dress in cold, rainy weather without hat or coat, he contracted pneumonia, and died one month to the day after his swearing in. His widow, Anna

Harrison, holds the distinction of being the First Lady in American history to receive a pension from Congress, receiving a year's worth of the salary Harrison would have earned had he lived. She was also exempted from paying for postage on any mail.

Memorable quote:

"Sir, I wish you to understand the true principles of the government. I wish them carried out. I ask nothing more."

--Final words of William Henry Harrison, as recorded by Jebediah Whitman.

Ten

John Tyler

(1790-1862)

Time in Office

(1841-1845)

John Tyler was born on March 29, 1790, to John
Tyler, Sr. and Mary Amistead, at his family's
Virginia plantation, called Greenway. Tyler's
background was similar to that of William Henry
Harrison's, as their family homes were located in
the same area of Virginia and their families
represented some of the oldest aristocratic
dynasties in the state. Tyler's father was close
friends and roommates with Thomas Jefferson,
and served in the Virginia legislature with
Harrison's father. Tyler's mother, also from a
prominent Virginia family, had eight children in
total, including three boys and five girls. She
died of a stroke in 1797, when Tyler was seven
years old. Tyler was considered sickly as a boy,
and probably suffered from what is now known
as Crohn's disease. He was educated at home by
private tutors until the age of twelve, when he
continued his family's tradition of studying at the
College of William and Mary in Williamsburg,

Virginia. Tyler graduated in 1807, at the age of seventeen, before studying law under the guidance of his father, as well as prominent Virginian Edmund Randolph. He was admitted to the bar at the age of nineteen, despite the fact that he was underage, because the examining judge neglected to ask him his age. Two years later, when he was 21, Tyler was elected to Virginia state legislature, beginning his political career.

In 1813, when Tyler was 23, he married Letitia Christian, who was also a member of a prominent Virginia family. The couple would go on to have eight children, and though Letitia lived long enough to become First Lady, she was unable to fulfill ceremonial functions due to the partial paralysis she suffered as a result of a stroke in 1839. Her daughter-in-law assumed her duties as Tyler's political hostess. Two years after Tyler became president, Letitia Tyler died after suffering a second stroke, making her the first First Lady to die while her husband was in office.

When John Tyler was remarried in 1844, to Julia Gardener of New York, who was thirty years younger than he, he became the first American president to marry while in office. Between the eight children from his first marriage and the seven children produced by his second marriage, Tyler holds the distinction of having fathered more legitimate children than any other president. Due to the late age at which he and his own sons fathered children, John Tyler still has two living grandsons as of 2018.

A committed member of the Democratic-Republican party, Tyler's politics were firmly in line with the agrarian, states' rights model established by Thomas Jefferson and James Madison during the early years of the republic. From 1811 to 1816, Tyler was a member of the Virginia state legislature. Afterwards, from 1817 to 1821, he served successive terms as a member of the U.S. House of Representatives, before returning to the Virginia legislature for two years in 1823. In 1825, he became governor of Virginia, delivering the eulogy at Thomas Jefferson's funeral in 1826. A year later, Tyler was elected to the Senate, where he served until 1836. During his career in the Senate, Tyler began to separate himself politically from fellow Democrat Andrew Jackson, whose closure of the national bank resulted in an unmitigated financial crisis and an official Congressional censure. When Tyler received instructions from his constituents in Virginia to vote for a repeal of the censure against Jackson, Tyler resigned from his Senate seat and joined the Whig party.

John Tyler was selected by the Whig party to be the running mate of William Henry Harrison during the presidential election of 1840. Tyler's political appeal lay in the fact that he was known to be a staunch supporter of states' rights, which would draw the Southern vote away from President Martin Van Buren. Harrison won a hands-down victory against Van Buren, only to develop a fatal case of pneumonia shortly after his inauguration. One month into office, he was dead, making John Tyler the first vice-president in American history to succeed the president before his term had expired. This triggered a governmental crisis, since the laws which govern the transfer of power to the vice-president in the event of a president's death or resignation were not formalized until the passage of the 25th Amendment to the Constitution in 1965.

Government leaders questioned whether Tyler was entitled to assume the full powers of the presidency, or whether he should simply preside ceremonially over the government while retaining only the powers of the vice-presidency. However, Tyler was duly sworn in as President two days after Harrison's death, on April 6, 1841. At the age of fifty-one, Tyler was the youngest person ever to become president. His political opponents swiftly dubbed him "His Accidency", referring to the unexpected manner of his becoming president. The nickname was also a reference to George Washington, who was addressed by Alexander Hamilton as "His

Excellency", a habit which Thomas Jefferson and others considered to be distastefully monarchial in tone.

Despite having been elected on the Whig ticket, Tyler quickly found himself at odds with Whig policy. Tyler inherited William Henry Harrison's cabinet, but the entire cabinet, with one exception, resigned from their positions after Tyler refused to authorize the creation of a new national bank. In 1843, the Whig party attempted, and failed, to impeach Tyler, making him, in effect, a president without a party. Despite this, Tyler's administration was not without significant accomplishments. During his term in office, American soldiers won the Seminole War in Florida, settlement of the western frontier was greatly expanded, and the lingering boundary dispute along the U.S.-Canadian border of Maine was resolved with the signing of the Webster Ashburton Treaty. Tyler was also the first president to make significant foreign policy strides in Asia, gaining American access to Chinese ports after the signing of the Treaty of Wanghia. Tyler's final contributions before leaving office were to sign the Congressional bill officially annexing the states of Texas and Florida into the Union. During the presidential election of 1844, Tyler attempted to run on a third-party ticket, but desisted early in the race when it became clear that he did not have enough support from either of the mainstream parties.

John Tyler spent the last eighteen years of his life with his second wife and their young family on their 1200-acre plantation, called Sherwood Forest, after the legendary site of the Robin Hood folk tales. He led a mostly retired existence until after the election of Abraham Lincoln in 1860, when he returned to Washington as part of an effort to broker a peace agreement between the northern and southern states. After the Civil War began with the firing of Confederate troops on Ft. Sumter, Tyler voted for Virginia's succession from the Union. Though he was elected to a seat in the Confederate House of Representatives, he died before assuming office, at the age of 71, in Richmond, Virginia. His death was not formally acknowledged by President Abraham Lincoln, who considered Tyler a traitor to his country. John Tyler was buried in Richmond, in the same cemetery as James Monroe, and later, Confederate president Jefferson Davis.

Memorable quote:

"Let it, then, be henceforth proclaimed to the world, that man's conscience was created free; that he is no longer accountable to his fellow man for his religious opinions, being responsible therefore only to his God."

--from John Tyler's funeral oration for Thomas Jefferson, 1826.

Eleven

James K. Polk

(1795-1849)

Time in Office

(1845-1849)

James Knox Polk was born on November 2, 1795, in a log cabin in Pineville, North Carolina, near present-day Charlotte. He was the oldest of ten children born to Samuel and Jane Knox Polk, moderately prosperous slave-owning farmers of Scotch-Irish descent whose forebears had immigrated to North America in the 1600s. In 1803, when Polk was eight years old, his grandfather moved the family to a new settlement in Maury County, Tennessee, where the Polk clan became deeply involved in local politics. Polk's father was known to socialize with

Andrew Jackson, who was working as a circuit court judge and lawyer in Tennessee at the time.

Polk suffered from poor health as a boy, which put his life at particular risk because there were few doctors in the frontier settlements where he grew up. In 1812, when Polk was seventeen, his father decided to take Polk to Philadelphia to be treated for kidney stones, but his condition worsened during the long journey, and a local doctor was forced to perform emergency surgery. Polk recovered and enjoyed good health afterwards, though it is thought that the surgery may have rendered him unable to have children of his own.

Polk's education was irregular in comparison to that of previous presidents. Regular schools were almost nonexistent in the western frontier at the time, so Polk's father offered to apprentice him in one of his businesses when he was eighteen. Polk instead chose to attend a local Presbyterian school, and then a school attached to the church he attended. After a few years' study at these schools and at Bradley Academy in Murfreesboro, Tennessee, Polk was judged a promising student, and admitted as a sophomore to the University of North Carolina at Chapel Hill, the nation's oldest public university. As a student there, Polk was a member of the Dialectic Society, where he honed his skills of debate and public oratory. After finishing his university studies, Polk returned to Tennessee, where he studied law under an attorney named Felix Grundy. While waiting to be admitted to the bar, Polk served as a clerk to the Tennessee legislature, a position he retained for several years, even after being granted his law license in 1820. In Polk's first criminal case, he defended his father Samuel after he was charged for brawling in public. He managed to secure his father's release for a fine of one dollar.

In 1823, after campaigning vigorously for a year, Polk was elected to the Tennessee legislature, where he served alongside Andrew Jackson. Two years later, Polk was elected to represent

Tennessee in Congress, and he remained a member of the House of Representatives until 1839, serving as Speaker of the House for the last four years of his Congressional career. On January 1, 1824, Polk was married to Sarah Childress, a member of the church he attended in Tennessee. Childress, who came from another prominent Tennessee political family, was unusually well-educated for a frontier woman in the early 19th century, and she played an active role in Polk's political career by reviewing his speeches, advising him on policy, and campaigning alongside him. When the couple moved to Washington, Sarah Polk established herself as a talented political hostess, which helped Polk make important alliances in the clannish world of Washington politics.

During the fourteen years Polk spent as a Congressional representative, he established himself as a supporter of "manifest destiny", the belief that white American settlers had a duty and a right to claim all of the North American territory for themselves, disregarding the rights of the indigenous inhabitants and other colonial powers who still had claims on the continent. He supported the proposed annexation of Texas and Oregon, which was among the most hotly contested issues in American politics during that time. By the time he returned to Tennessee in 1840 to become the state's governor, his reputation was well-established in the Democratic party, and Andrew Jackson had adopted him as a protégée. During Jackson's presidency, Polk supported him staunchly during the crisis over the closing of the Second Bank of the United States and the Panic of 1837 which followed. Likewise, Polk supported Jackson when John C. Calhoun of South Carolina threatened succession over the so-called "Tariff of Abominations", and favored Jackson's proposal to send federal troops to South Carolina to force compliance with federal law.

In 1840, Polk returned to Tennessee to become the state's governor. Four years later, during the presidential election of 1844, Polk emerged as the leading Democratic candidate for his party's nomination, despite opposition from fellow Democrat and former president Martin Van Buren. Polk's nomination was supported by Andrew Jackson, who favored Polk's positive stance on the annexation of Texas. Westward expansion and manifest destiny appealed to the imagination of the American people at the time, and as a result Polk defeated Whig opponent Henry Clay by a significant electoral margin, though the popular vote was more evenly divided.

When Polk was sworn into office on March 4, 1845, he became the youngest president in American history at the age of 49. His was also the first inaugural address ever reported live via telegraph to the international press. In the final days of President John Tyler's administration, Texas accepted the offer of U.S. annexation. As a result, Polk took office having inherited an imminent threat of war with Mexico, which severed diplomatic ties with the U.S. on the basis of the fact that Mexico continued to regard Texas as a Mexican province in rebellion against its rightful government. Relations between the United States and England were also strained during this time, as England had made claims on portions of the Oregon territory some thirty years earlier. The Oregon territory then encompassed a much larger tract of land than the present-day state of Oregon, and would have expanded American borders up the Pacific coast as far north as Alaska, into present-day Canada. Many of Polk's political allies were prepared to go to war to retain the American claim on the Oregon territory, but Polk, unwilling to enter yet another armed conflict against the British, negotiated a permanent border between Canada and the United States along the 49th parallel, which stands to this day.

In 1845, as tensions escalated along the Texas-Mexico border, Polk dispatched American troops under the command of General Zachary Taylor to southern Texas, with orders to defend American territory in Texas and dissuade the Mexicans from making military advances, while meeting any show of force with proportional armed response. Even after Polk offered to compensate Mexico for the loss of Texas, war was inevitable, as American soldiers were occupying disputed territory between the Texan and Mexican borders. In 1846, when negotiations with Texas failed after a military coup took over the Mexican government, Polk ordered American troops under Zachary Taylor to hold and defend all land north of the Rio Grande river. In May of the same year, Congress officially declared war against Mexico, after American soldiers clashed with Mexican troops in a skirmish that crossed to the American side of the Rio Grande border.

The Mexican-American War lasted until 1848, when hostilities ceased after the signing of the Treaty of Guadalupe Hidalgo. During the last year of Polk's administration, he signed legislation prohibiting slavery in the Oregon territory in accordance with the boundary lines established by the Missouri Compromise. Polk, who had run for president on the pledge that he would only seek one term in office, did not run for re-election in 1848. He was succeeded in office by Whig candidate Zachary Taylor, who had become popular throughout the country as a hero of the late war.

After leaving office, James and Sarah Polk embarked on a tour of the country, intending to retire from public life afterwards. During the tour, Polk, whose health had grown weak during his years in the White House, was exposed to an outbreak of cholera. He appeared to recover from the illness, only to suffer a fatal relapse shortly after settling in at Polk Place in Tennessee, the house he had prepared for his family after his retirement. He died, surrounded by family and doctors, on June 15, 1849. Polk survived only 103 days after the end of his presidency, making him the shortest-lived of all former presidents, apart from those who died before leaving office. He was buried in Nashville, though his remains, and those of his wife, were later removed to the Tennessee State Capitol.

Memorable quote:

"But it is, in point of fact, untrue that an act passed by Congress is conclusive evidence that it is an emanation of the popular will. A majority of the whole number elected to each House of Congress constitutes a quorum, and a majority of that quorum is competent to pass laws. It might happen that a quorum of the House of Representatives, consisting of a single member more than half of the whole number elected to that House, might pass a bill by a majority of a single vote, and in that case a fraction more than one-fourth of the people of the United States would be represented by those who voted for it. It might happen that the same bill might be passed by a majority of one of a quorum of the Senate, composed of senators from the fifteen smaller States, and a single senator from a sixteenth State, and if the senators voting for it happened to be from the eight of the smallest of these States, it would be passed by the votes of senators from States having but fourteen representatives in the House of Representatives, and containing less than one-sixteenth of the whole population of the United States. This extreme case is stated to illustrate the fact, that the mere passage of a bill by Congress is no conclusive evidence that those who passed it represent the majority of the people of the United States, or truly reflect their will. If such an extreme case is not likely to happen, cases that approximate it are of constant occurrence. It is believed that not a single law has been passed, since the adoption of the constitution, upon which all the members elected to both Houses have been present and voted. Many of the most important acts which have passed Congress have been carried by a close vote in thin Houses. Many instances of this might be given. Indeed, our experience proves that many of the most important acts of Congress are postponed to the last days, and often the last hours of a session, when they are disposed of in haste, and by Houses but little exceeding the number necessary to form a quorum."

--James K. Polk, from his Fourth Annual Message to Congress, 1848

Twelve

Zachary Taylor

(1784-1850)

Time in Office

(1849-1850)

Zachary Taylor was born on November 24, 1784, to Richard and Sarah Dabney Taylor, on one of his family's plantations in present-day Orange County, Virginia. Taylor was one of five brothers, only three of whom lived to adulthood, and he also had three younger sisters. On his father's side, Taylor was descended from William Brewster, a prominent early American settler who came to North America on the *Mayflower* and helped settle Plymouth Colony in Massachusetts. When Taylor was very young, his family left Virginia, where their fortunes were in decline, and moved to Louisville, Kentucky, where Taylor spent the rest of his childhood. Though at first the Taylor family lived in a remote log cabin, Richard Taylor eventually expanded his holdings in Kentucky to include 10,000 acres of land and at least 26 slaves. His family moved to a respectable brick home in the booming city of Louisville, though Taylor was able to gain only a sporadic education due to the primitive frontier conditions common in Kentucky at the time. Taylor studied with private tutors, including his mother, who taught him how to read and write, and later attended a small academy run by an Irish educator who gave Taylor a basic grounding in the classics. In 1810, at the age of 26, Taylor married Margaret McCall Smith, who came from a wealthy family of

Maryland planters. Smith's father, like Taylor's, had served as an officer during the Revolutionary War. The couple went on to have five daughters and one son, though two of their daughters died in early childhood as a result of a "bilious fever".

From a young age, Taylor's ambition was for a military career, and due to his legendary service in the Mexican-American War and the short duration of his presidency, it is his military career which offers the most scope for biographical interest. Taylor received his first commission in 1808, as the commander of the garrison at Fort Pickering, near present-day Memphis, Tennessee. By the time of his marriage in 1810, Taylor was promoted to captain and assigned to the command of the fort at Baton Rouge, Louisiana, where he was joined by his family. During this period, he increased his personal fortunes through a number of successful land speculations throughout Kentucky, Mississippi, and other parts of the south. In 1811, he briefly held command of Fort

Knox, in what was then part of the Indiana Territory. He remained in the Indiana Territory after the outbreak of the War of 1812. After successfully defending Fort Harrison against attack, Taylor was given the first brevet promotion in American military history, to the rank of major. As brevet promotions are temporary promotions given in the field during time of war, Taylor was demoted to captain when the war ended in 1815, but was permanently promoted to major shortly afterwards.

For the next thirteen years, Taylor received steady promotions and assignments of increasing importance and responsibility throughout the western American frontier. In 1828, after being promoted to the rank of colonel, he took command of the 1st Infantry Regiment of the American army for the duration of the Black Hawk War again the Sauk Indian leader Black Hawk, heading a large coalition of Indian nations against the encroachment of white settlers on native lands. Both Abraham

Lincoln and Jefferson Davis also fought in the Black Hawk War. Jefferson Davis, who was close to Taylor, asked permission to marry Taylor's 17-year old daughter, Sarah, permission which Taylor denied because he did not wish for his daughter to suffer the irregular existence of a military wife. Sarah and Davis eloped against his wishes and were married for three months before she died suddenly of malaria.

Zachary Taylor gained the nickname "Old Rough and Ready" during the Second Seminole War, which began in 1838. Now a brigadier general, Taylor was responsible for defeating the largest force of Indian fighters in the history of the 19th century American genocide of the native population. Taylor was enormously popular amongst American soldiers because he rejected the trappings and privileges of his rank and openly shared the hardships of field duty with the enlisted men. After the war, Taylor took a year's furlough and toured the United States to confer with other high-ranking military leaders.

For the next several years, until the outbreak of the Mexican-American War, Taylor met and corresponded with individuals such as William Henry Harrison, and began to take an interest in national politics.

In 1844, President James K. Polk ordered Taylor to defend Louisiana against a possible Mexican invasion of the United States, and later in 1846 placed him at the head of the Army of Occupation, with instructions to position himself "on or near the Rio Grande" in an effort to intimidate Mexico into ceasing hostilities. When negotiations with Mexico failed, Taylor won several decisive victories against Mexican forces, including the Battle of Palo Alto, the Battle of Resaca de Palma, the Battle of Monterrey, and the Battle of Buena Vista, which brought the war to an end. Serving under Taylor at this time were a large number of officers who would later become major figures on both sides of the Civil War, including Ulysses S. Grant, who admired Taylor enormously and would model his style of command after Taylor's. Taylor won nationwide popularity during the war due not only to the role he played in the American victory, but also because of his humane treatment of Mexican prisoners of war, ensuring that they were fed, their wounded cared for, and that the dying received the last rites of the Catholic church. In 1848, Taylor returned to Louisiana, where he was greeted by cheering crowds.

Though the prospect of Taylor's running for president had been raised during the war, Taylor had responded with skepticism, claiming that it was something neither he nor any sane person would think of. His politics were not entirely aligned with either the Democratic or Whig parties, though he had allies on both sides. As a slave-owner, he was popular with southerners, while northerners respected his storied military career, and were reassured by his opposition to southern secession and the expansion of slavery. Though he disagreed with major issues on the Whig platform, and considered himself a

Jeffersonian democrat at heart, Taylor's Whig supporters spent two years persuading him to allow himself to be nominated at the convention of 1848, where he defeated Henry Clay and Winfield Scot for the candidacy. During the national election, Taylor won a decisive victory against Martin Van Buren, running for the Free Soil Party, and Lewis Cass, the Democratic candidate. Zachary Taylor's election as the twelfth president of the United States marked the last occasion in the nation's history in which a third-party candidate was elected. Taylor would also be the last southern president until Woodrow Wilson's election in 1912.

Taylor's brief presidency was dominated by the issue of slavery expansion. Though a slave-owner himself, he opposed the expansion of slavery into new American states and territories, especially Texas, and supported the Wilmot Proviso, which would forbid slavery in Oregon. Threats of southern secession grew even more pronounced as Taylor's southern supporters came to regard him as a traitor to their cause. The secession question built to its penultimate crisis in February of 1850, and Taylor made clear that he would regard any attempts at secession as a form of rebellion against the Union, and that those responsible would be hanged "with less reluctance than he had hanged deserters and spies in Mexico."

Taylor had become ill during a pre-inaugural tour of the country, conducted in inclement weather. His health never recovered, and in July of 1850, after sixteen months in office, he died unexpectedly at the age of 65, after complaining of pains in his stomach. He was posthumously diagnosed with a form of cholera by his doctors. Taylor was succeeded in office by his vice-president, Millard Fillmore. He was buried in the Congressional Cemetery in Washington, D.C., before his remains were moved to his family home in Kentucky.

Memorable quote:

"In conclusion I congratulate you, my fellow-citizens, upon the high state of prosperity to which the goodness of Divine Providence has conducted our common country. Let us invoke a continuance of the same protecting care which has led us from small beginnings to the eminence we this day occupy."

--from Zachary Taylor's inaugural address, 1849.

Thirteen

Millard Fillmore

(1800-1874)

Time in Office

(1850-1853)

Millard Fillmore was born on January 7, 1800, to parents Phoebe Millard and Nathaniel Fillmore, the second of their eight children and their oldest son. The Fillmore family was descended from English settlers in the Connecticut area, and several of Fillmore's male relatives had fought in the American Revolution. Millard Fillmore enjoys the distinction of being one of the few presidents who was actually born in a log cabin, on his family's property in Cayuga County, New York, which is part of the Finger Lakes region. He was also the first American president born in the 19th century.

When Fillmore was a boy, his father found that the title to his land was defective, and was forced to move to a nearby town where he worked as a tenant farmer and occasional schoolteacher. Fillmore received virtually no formal schooling as a boy; his father's goal was for his oldest son to learn a trade that would enable him to make a comfortable living. When Fillmore attempted to enlist in the army during the War of 1812, his father instead persuaded him to start an apprenticeship under a local cloth merchant. Fillmore, however, was eager to become educated, and read books from his local circulating library during his scant free time. At the age of 19, he quit his job at a local mill and enrolled in an academy, where he met and fell in love with Abigail Powers, a classmate who was training to become a teacher. Before the couple married, however, Fillmore began studying law under the guidance of Judge Walter Wood, who was also his father's landlord. Though Fillmore worked as Wood's clerk, Wood did not pay him, and the two quarreled and parted ways after Fillmore gave legal advice to a local farmer before receiving his license to practice. After reaching his majority at the age of 21, Fillmore began working as a school teacher, before moving to Buffalo and continuing to study. After being admitted to the New York state bar in 1823, he moved to the small town of East Aurora. In 1826, he and Abigail Powers married. They had two children, a son and a daughter.

Two years later, Fillmore became a member of the Anti-Masonic Party, a proto-libertarian political organization opposed to the perceived elitism of societies such as the Freemasons. He campaigned unsuccessfully for the re-election of President John Quincy Adams, and was elected to the New York state legislature in 1828, serving from 1829 to 1831. As a state legislator, one of his accomplishments was abolishing the practice of making witnesses swear religious oaths before giving testimony in court, and repealing laws that allowed for debtors to be imprisoned for their debts. After resigning from the state legislature in 1831, Fillmore ran for Congress the following year. He was elected, and served four terms in total, and though his bid to become Speaker of the House in his fourth term was unsuccessful, he was appointed head of the influential Ways and Means Committee. In 1843, he resigned from Congress in order to run for the governor's seat in New York. He was defeated, and returned to private life with his family in Buffalo, serving as New York comptroller until the presidential election of 1848, when he was selected as candidate Zachary Taylor's running mate.

Fillmore's working class northern background and strong ties to the business community were thought to balance Taylor's southern roots, his military background, and his status as a slave-owner. During his brief vice-presidency, Fillmore presided over the Senate, making him an influential figure during the contentious slavery debates that dominated American politics during that decade. In January of 1850, Kentucky senator Henry Clay introduced an ambitious compromise bill which called for California to be admitted to the Union as a free state, banned the slave trade (though not slavery itself) in the District of Columbia, and authorized the establishment territorial government in the newly-acquired territories of New Mexico and Utah, where decisions about the future of slavery would be decided by popular sovereignty. Clay's bill also called for mandatory enforcement of the Fugitive Slave Act, which required persons in the northern states to assist in the recapture and relocation of slaves who had escaped their southern owners. Neither northern nor southern politicians were entirely satisfied by the compromise bill, and Fillmore himself did not approve of it, but after presiding over heated debates, Fillmore informed President Taylor that, if the vote were tied, he would, as President of the Senate, break the tie in favor of the bill. Debate continued for another five months, until Zachary Taylor's abrupt death on July 9, 1850.

Fillmore was unaware that Taylor was seriously ill until only a few hours before Taylor's death made him the thirteenth president of the United States. Traditionally, when presidents leave office or are elected to a second term, their entire cabinet offers their resignation, with the expectation that their resignations will be refused. Fillmore, however, became the first and only vice-president to succeed to office due to the death or resignation of his predecessor who accepted the cabinet resignations, filling the newly vacated posts with Whig politicians who had supported him as vice-president. With Fillmore's public support, Henry Clay's compromise bill was adopted and signed into law, becoming known as the Compromise of 1850. It was to be the one significant achievement of his presidency. During Fillmore's administration, California was admitted to the Union as a free state, and the slave trade, though not slavery itself, was outlawed in Washington. Despite Fillmore's personal anti-slavery stance, he authored federal officers to enforce the Fugitive Slave Act in the northern states where the law was unpopular and often flouted. Such contradictory stances earned him enemies both amongst southerners and among northern abolitionists. Rather than building coalitions which would help him gain a second term in office, he focused on maintaining national unity to the extent possible during the decade leading up to the Civil War.

After Fillmore completed Zachary Taylor's term of office, the Whig party chose not to nominate him for the 1852 presidential election, instead supporting General Winfield Scott, who lost to Democratic candidate Franklin Pierce. Over the next few years, the Whig part lost cohesion and disintegrated into new factions, including the vehemently anti-slavery Republican Party. Fillmore's personal life was in some disarray after his departure from Washington, as he was the only former president to leave office without having become independently wealthy or having a family estate to return to. He determined to begin practicing law again, though his plans were halted briefly when his wife, who had taken a cold during Franklin Pierce's inauguration, died of pneumonia in 1853, and their daughter Mary died of cholera the next spring. During the presidential election of 1856, when the American political landscape was fracturing into multiple political parties, all of which reflected various contradictory stances on the slavery question, Fillmore accepted the nomination of the so-called Know-Nothing Party, only to be defeated by James Buchanan. Fillmore retired from politics and married again to a wealthy widow named Caroline McIntosh. With his financial troubles behind him, Fillmore became a noted charitable philanthropist.

In the years prior to the Civil War, Fillmore was a committed anti-secessionist who criticized President James Buchanan for not taking stronger measures against the discontented southern states. He was also a vocal critic of President Abraham Lincoln, supporting Stephen Douglas during the 1860 presidential election, and George McClellan, Lincoln's opponent for the Republican nomination, during the 1864 election. Fillmore shared McClellan's belief that the Civil War could only be brought to an end if a peace agreement were negotiated which would allow the southern states to keep their slaves. Despite this opposition, Fillmore was among the delegation of Buffalo citizens who accompanied Lincoln's funeral procession during its national progress to Illinois. Fillmore spent the final decade of his life participating in local civic government, and died in 1874 after suffering two strokes in February and March of that year. He was buried in Forest Lawn Cemetery, in Buffalo, New York.

Memorable quotes:

"Let us remember that revolutions do not always establish freedom. Our own free institutions were not the offspring of our Revolution. They existed before. They were planted in the free charters of self-government under which the English colonies grew up, and our Revolution only freed us from the dominion of a foreign power whose government was at variance with those institutions. But European nations have had no such training for self-government, and every effort to establish it by bloody revolutions has been, and must, without that preparation, continue to be a failure. Liberty, unregulated by law, degenerates into anarchy, which soon becomes the most horrid of all despotisms. Our policy is wisely to govern ourselves, and thereby to set such an example of national justice, prosperity, and true glory, as shall teach to all nations the blessings of self-government, and the unparalleled enterprise and success of a free people."

--from Millard Fillmore's Third Annual Message to Congress, 1852.

Fourteen

Franklin Pierce

(1804-1869)

Time in Office

(1853-1857)

Franklin Pierce was born in Hillsborough, New Hampshire, on November 23, 1804, the fifth of eight children born to Benjamin and Anna

Kendrick Pierce. Benjamin Pierce had been a lieutenant in Massachusetts during the Revolutionary War, but had relocated to New Hampshire after the war's end, purchasing fifty acres of land on which to establish a farm. On his father's side, Franklin Pierce was descended from founding members of the Massachusetts Bay Colony, who settled in New England in 1634.

Benjamin Pierce, who was active in local politics, prioritized the educations of his sons. Pierce was sent to school in Hillsborough, and later in Hancock, a distance of some twelve miles from his family's home. At first a reluctant student who suffered from homesickness, Pierce eventually began to take his studies seriously, transferring to Phillips Exeter Academy in order to prepare academically for Bowdoin College in Maine, where he became a student in 1820. While at Bowdoin, Pierce became friends with American novelist Nathaniel Hawthorne, and the two remained close throughout their lives. Pierce graduated from Bowdoin in 1824, placing fifth out of the fourteen graduating members of his class. During his university career, Pierce took an active part in literary societies, as well as an unofficial student militia calling itself the Bowdoin Cadets.

After leaving college, Pierce worked a schoolteacher in Hebron, Maine, for several months before studying law with Levi Woodbury, a friend of the Pierce family and former governor of New Hampshire. Unusually for many American lawyers in the early 19th century, Pierce also studied for a semester at Northampton Law School in Massachusetts. He was admitted to the New Hampshire bar in 1827, where he began his law practice with partner Albert Baker, brother of Mary Baker Eddy, the founder of the Christian Science movement.

Pierce was drawn out of law and into politics after his father was elected governor of New Hampshire in 1827. Pierce, who was young, handsome, and known for his charming manners and excellent speaking voice, won his first election, as town moderator for the city of Hillsborough, a position to which he would be re-elected for the following six years. In 1828, he was elected to the New Hampshire state legislature, where he was eventually elected Speaker of the House. Though satisfied with his professional career, Pierce was impatient with state politics, and with being a bachelor. On November 19, 1834, Pierce married Jane Means Appleton, daughter of a former president of Bowdoin College. The couple would have three sons, all of whom died in childhood.

Just before his marriage, Pierce was elected to the U.S. House of Representatives, where he served for one term before resigning and being elected to the Senate from 1837 to 1842. Pierce enjoyed popularity in Washington, but Jane Pierce was uncomfortable in the city, prompting Pierce's decision to return to New Hampshire and resume his law practice. A member of the state militia, Pierce was promoted to brigadier general during the Mexican-American War, and during the decade after the war's end, he did not seek public office. Still an active member of the New Hampshire Democratic party, Pierce played a role in organizing support for various candidates, such as Lewis Cass, who ran for president during the 1848 election. He was also known for his public support of the Compromise of 1850, upholding the Fugitive Slave Act, to the dismay of northern abolitionists. Pierce's status as a northerner willing to compromise with the south on slavery-related issues garnered him a strong support base, and in 1852, he was nominated during the Democratic National Convention to be the party's candidate in the upcoming presidential election, defeating established national figures such as Stephen A. Douglas and James Buchanan. While the Democratic party was unified in its support for the Compromise of 1850, the Whig party was divided between compromise supporters, abolitionists, and southern supporters of slavery expansion, enabling Pierce to win a narrow victory over Whig candidate General Winfield Scott.

Two months before Pierce's inauguration as president, his last surviving child, Bennie, who was eleven, was killed in a train wreck. Jane Pierce, who had not wanted her husband to run for president in the first place, suffered deeply from the loss and spent the first two years of her tenure as First Lady in secluded mourning. Pierce's inauguration was unique in several ways: he was, at 49, the youngest president ever elected, and he was the first president apart from John Quincy Adams to swear his oath of office on a book of law rather than on a copy of the Bible. He was also the first president to deliver his inaugural address from memory.

Pierce began his administration optimistic that the debate around slavery had been effectively settled by the Compromise of 1850. His inaugural address expressed his hope that "the [slavery] question is at rest". This would prove to be anything but the case. Expanding the nation's borders was a popular cause amongst slavery expansionists, and some of Pierce's foreign policy initiatives, such as his efforts to negotiate with Spain for the purchase of Cuba, aroused the suspicions of northern abolitionists. The 1853 Gadsden Purchase, orchestrated by Pierce's secretary of war Jefferson Davis, involved the purchase of land from Mexico that would enable the construction of a railway line which would connect the American south with the Pacific southwest. Other attempts at land acquisition included the events leading to the Ostend Manifesto, in which the United States formally announced that it would regard itself as justified in seizing Cuba from the Spanish if the American government determined that Spain was undermining American national security.

The most significant event of Franklin Pierce's administration was the passage of the Kansas-Nebraska Act, one of the most serious precipitating factors of the Civil War. The Act was proposed to Congress by Kentucky senator

Stephen A. Douglas in 1854, proposing that Kansas and Nebraska be divided into separate territories open to American settlement, and that the legality of slavery in those territories be determined by popular sovereignty—that is, by the inhabitants of the territories themselves, rather than by Congress. Effectively, this opened Kansas to the slave trade, in contravention of the Missouri Compromise of 1820. Pierce supported Douglas's agenda, despite opposition from abolitionists, the Free Soil Party, and the newly formed Republican Party. A phenomenon known as "Bleeding Kansas" was the result. Most Kansans were opposed to slavery, but slavery expansionists from across the Missouri border poured into the state to sway the vote, and since there was no means of verifying their actual place of residence, there was no effective means of keeping them away from the polls. By 1855, the Kansas legislature was filled with pro-slavery delegates, and the anti-slavery settlers protested by attempting to establish a rival government. Violence broke out, not only in Kansas, but on the floor of Congress, after a South Carolina Congressman physically assaulted northern abolitionist Senator Charles Sumner, who asserted publically that southern slave-owners were prone to raping their female slaves. The scandal proved to be the end of Pierce's political career. During the 1856 Democratic National Convention, Pierce was not nominated for re-election; James Buchanan was nominated in his place, becoming president in 1857.

Franklin remained in Washington for two months after the end of his administration, and spent the next three years traveling in warmer climates for the sake of his wife's health. As the Civil War loomed nearer, Franklin was openly critical of northern abolitionists, accusing them of inciting southern slavery expansionists towards secession and war. He was no less critical of President Abraham Lincoln after the outbreak of war, denouncing the Emancipation Proclamation as a divisive act that would make peace with the south impossible. After the death of Jane Pierce in 1863, Pierce retired from politics and public life. He became a heavy drinker in his final years. When Confederate president Jefferson Davis was arrested at the end of the Civil War, Pierce exerted his remaining influence to ameliorate the conditions of Davis's imprisonment. Alienated from his surviving family, Pierce died in Concord, New Hampshire, on October 8, 1869, of cirrhosis of the liver, attended only by a hired caretaker. He was buried in Concord near his wife and two older sons.

Memorable quotes:

"The storm of frenzy and faction must inevitably dash itself in vain against the unshaken rock of the Constitution. I shall never doubt it. I know that the Union is stronger a thousand times than all the wild and chimerical schemes of social change which are generated one after another in the unstable minds of visionary sophists and interested agitators. I rely confidently on the patriotism of the people, on the dignity and self-respect of the States, on the wisdom of Congress, and, above all, on the continued gracious favor of Almighty God to maintain against all enemies, whether at home or abroad, the sanctity of the Constitution and the integrity of the Union."

--from Franklin Pierce's Third Annual Message to Congress, 1855.

Fifteen

James Buchanan

(1791-1868)

Time in Office

(1857-1861)

James Buchanan was born on April 23, 1791, in a log cabin in Cove Gap, Pennsylvania. He was the fifteenth American president, and the last to have been born in the 18th century. Buchanan's father, James Sr., emigrated to North America from Ireland; his mother, Elizabeth Speer, was uncommonly well-educated for a woman of her background. James Buchanan was the first of the couple's eleven children to survive infancy.

When Buchanan was a young boy his family moved to Mercersburg, Pennsylvania, where his father's business ventures met with considerable success, making him the wealthiest man in town. Buchanan was one of the few early 19th century American presidents to attend school regularly as a boy, studying at the Old Stone Academy in Mercersburg until he was admitted to Dickinson College in Carlisle, Pennsylvania, at the age of sixteen. He was considered intelligent but undisciplined, and was nearly expelled for unruly conduct before graduating with honors in 1809. After graduation, he moved to Lancaster, then the capital of Pennsylvania, where he began to study law under the guidance of a local lawyer named James Hopkins. Buchanan was admitted to the Pennsylvania bar in 1812, after which he opened his own practice.

In 1814, at the age of 23, Buchanan was elected to the Pennsylvania state legislature, where he served until 1816. Four years later, he was elected to national office for the first time, as a member of the U.S. House of Representatives. Buchanan's Congressional career spanned the next ten years, during which time he became an established member of the new Democratic Party. In 1831, during President Andrew Jackson's administration, Buchanan was appointed the American ambassador to Russia, in which capacity he negotiated important trade treaties with the government of Tsar Nicholas I.

When Buchanan was twenty-eight, he was briefly engaged to Ann Coleman, who belonged to a wealthy Pennsylvania manufacturing family, but the wedding was called off shortly before Coleman's unexpected death, which was rumored to be a suicide. He was to become the first unmarried American president, and during his administration the ceremonial duties of First Lady were fulfilled by his niece, Harriet Lane.

Buchanan returned to the United States from Russia in 1834, at which point he was elected to the U.S. Senate, although he resigned after only two years, when President James K. Polk appointed him to his cabinet as secretary of state. During Polk's administration, U.S. borders were expanded to the Pacific Coast, and the nation gained territorial acquisitions amounting to more than a third of its previous size, all overseen by Buchanan. Like Franklin Pierce, Buchanan was a northerner sympathetic to southern interests regarding slavery, and he was an open supporter of the Compromise of 1850. During Pierce's presidency, Buchanan was honored with the appointment of ambassador to England, where he helped to draft the Ostend Manifesto, declaring America's intention to seize Cuba in the event that the Spanish attempted to infringe upon American sovereignty.

Pierce's presidency and political career foundered in 1856, as a result of the disastrous and violent consequences of the Kansas-Nebraska Act, and he did not receive his party's nomination during that year's presidential election. Instead, the nomination settled on Buchanan, whose reputation had not suffered from association with the Kansas-Nebraska Act, since he was abroad in Great Britain at the time it was being debated. Buchanan, who believed that it should be left to individual states and territories to decide whether or not to adopt slavery, was elected with a simple majority over the candidates from the Republican, Free Soil, and "Know-Nothing" Parties. His running mate was 35-year old Kentucky Congressman John Breckenridge, who became the youngest vice-president in American history after Buchanan's election.

Like previous presidents during the decade preceding the Civil War, Buchanan's principle concern was to keep the peace between north and south. But he was increasingly perceived as being pro-slavery and pro-southern, particularly after the U.S. Supreme Court handed down its ruling in the famous Dred Scott case, in which Scott, a slave, attempted to sue his owners for his freedom after they transported him from the south to Illinois, where slavery was illegal. The court ruled that as Scott was "a negro of the African race" he had no standing as a citizen in the United States and therefore could not bring suit in federal court. The court also found that the federal government had no legal grounds to enforce anti-slavery laws in the western territories. Both Buchanan and the supreme justice of the court had believed that the decision would quell debate over slavery, but the result was just the opposite, with tensions becoming only further inflamed. When Buchanan voiced his support of the Lecompton Constitution, which would have permitted slavery in Kansas, he further alienated northerners. In 1858, anti-slavery Republicans won a majority in the U.S.

Congress, effectively stalemating Buchanan's legislative agenda.

In accordance with a promise made during his 1857 inaugural address, Buchanan chose not to run for a second term in office during the election of 1860. The Democratic nomination went to Stephen A. Douglas of Illinois, while the Republican nomination was given to Abraham Lincoln, also of Illinois. The state of South Carolina declared its intent to secede from the Union should Lincoln be elected, and on December 20, 1860, the secession was announced. Six more states would secede between the day of Lincoln's election and his first day in office. Buchanan would later be held to blame by future presidents for not taking more vigorous action to prevent succession. He felt that, while no state had a right to secede, he, as president, was not authorized by the Constitution to prevent them from doing so. Buchanan confessed himself relieved to be leaving office and handing the nation's problems over to a new administration.

Despite this, Buchanan openly supported President Lincoln during the war years. Most of the remainder of his life was spent defending his reputation against those who blamed him for the outbreak of the war. To this end, he published a memoir in 1866, entitled *Mr. Buchanan's Administration on the Eve of Rebellion.* Emotionally disturbed by attacks on his character, which included being burned in effigy, Buchanan remained in poor health until 1868, when he caught a cold and began to suffer from respiratory failure. He died on June 1, 1868, at the age of 77, and was buried near his home in Lancaster, Pennsylvania.

Memorable quote:

"All agree that under the Constitution slavery in the States is beyond the reach of any human power except that of the respective States themselves wherein it exists. May we not, then, hope that the long agitation on this subject is approaching its end, and that the geographical parties to which it has given birth, so much dreaded by the Father of his Country, will speedily become extinct? Most happy will it be for the country when the public mind shall be diverted from this question to others of more pressing and practical importance. Throughout the whole progress of this agitation, which has scarcely known any intermission for more than twenty years, whilst it has been productive of no positive good to any human being it has been the prolific source of great evils to the master, to the slave, and to the whole country. It has alienated and estranged the people of the sister States from each other, and has even seriously endangered the very existence of the Union. Nor has the danger yet entirely ceased. Under our system there is a remedy for all mere political evils in the sound sense and sober judgment of the people. Time is a great corrective. Political subjects which but a few years ago excited and exasperated the public mind have passed away and are now nearly forgotten. But this question of domestic slavery is of far graver importance than any mere political question, because should the agitation continue it may eventually endanger the personal safety of a large portion of our countrymen where the institution exists. In that event no form of government, however admirable in itself and however productive of material benefits, can compensate for the loss of peace and domestic security around the family altar. Let every Union-loving man, therefore, exert his best influence to suppress this agitation, which since the recent legislation of Congress is without any legitimate object."

--from James Buchanan's inaugural address, 1857.

Part Four: The Civil War

Sixteen

Abraham Lincoln

(1809-1865)

Time in Office

(1861-1865)

Abraham Lincoln was born to Thomas and Nancy Hanks Lincoln on February 12, 1809, in a log cabin on Sinking Springs farm in rural western Kentucky. He had a sister, Sarah, who was two years older than him, and would have a younger brother, Thomas, who died as an infant. When Lincoln was seven years old, his father moved the family to Indiana, where Nancy Lincoln died of an infection caused by drinking contaminated milk. The following year, Thomas Lincoln married Sarah Bush Johnston, a widow who had three children from her previous marriage. Lincoln had a difficult relationship with his father throughout his life, but he was close to his step-mother, who encouraged his desire to receive an education.

In the early 19th century, children did not become legally independent of their fathers until they were 21 years old, and it was not uncommon for parents to send their children to neighboring towns and farms to earn money for the family. Until he turned 21, Lincoln was obligated to work on his father's behalf. His formal education was sporadic even by the standards of the western frontier, where schools were rare, but Lincoln frequently borrowed books from neighbors, or rented them in return for labor. In his youth, Lincoln gained a reputation for being able to read and write in a fluent, professional manner, and his family's neighbors frequently asked him for his help with deciphering and understanding important correspondence. Lincoln sometimes suffered from depression as a young man, due in part to his father's harsh treatment and his own aspirations for a career other than subsistence farming. After his brief engagement to a young women ended in her unexpected death, Lincoln's friends became concerned that he was suicidal. In 1830, shortly before Lincoln turned 21, his family moved to Illinois, and Lincoln took a job on a flatboat that transported goods down the Mississippi River. He thought of running away in order to be free of his father's control, but was advised by a relative that he would risk getting himself into legal difficulties by doing so. During his first trip south, the young Lincoln encountered a slave auction for the first time, an experience which disturbed him deeply and influenced the development of his opinions on slavery.

Lincoln's family moved away from Illinois when he was 21, but Lincoln remained in the state, taking a job at a general store in New Salem and serving for a time as a postmaster. In 1832, after the outbreak of the Black Hawk War, Lincoln joined a militia, and was elected captain. His regiment never saw combat, and this was to be the only military experience of Lincoln's life. When the war ended, Lincoln returned to civilian life and made his first unsuccessful bid at entering politics, running for a seat in the Illinois state legislature. Afterwards, he began studying law. Most lawyers of the era obtained a university degree in the classics before studying law privately under the guidance of an established older lawyer in the community, but this option was not available to Lincoln, who instead purchased, borrowed, and leased law books wherever they were available and studied entirely on his own. In 1834, Lincoln was elected to the Illinois legislature, and in 1836 he was admitted to the Illinois bar, after which he began to practice law with John Stuart Todd. In 1842, Lincoln married Todd's cousin, Mary. The couple would have four sons, though only the oldest, Robert Todd Lincoln, would survive to adulthood.

Lincoln's legislative career in Illinois lasted for several terms. A faithful member of the Whig party before its dissolution, his chief political focus was on improving infrastructure in the western frontier, to reduce the isolation of outlying settlements. He was also part of the movement that led to the city of Springfield being named the new capital of Illinois. In 1846, Lincoln was elected to national office for the first time, gaining a seat in the U.S. House of Representatives. His Congressional career was short-lived, however, as he was not elected to a second term, due to his unpopular stance opposing the Mexican-American War.

For the next several years, Lincoln focused on building his law practice and raising his family. He remained active in local Whig politics, aided by the connections he gained through Mary Todd Lincoln's affluent family. In 1857, Lincoln refused a seat in the state legislature because he hoped that the Illinois Assembly would elect him to the U.S. Senate. (Senatorial elections were often held by state legislatures before the 17th Amendment, which provides for the direct election of U.S. senators, was passed.) Lincoln lost the election for the senate by dropping out of the race and swinging his votes towards another member of the Whig party, to prevent the election of a Democrat.

Lincoln, like many white settlers on the western frontier, had never owned slaves, and like most northern Whigs, he was politically opposed to the expansion of slavery. In the 1850s, however, abolitionists—those who believed in an immediate, universal end to slavery—were considered radicals, and were often subject to punitive mob violence. Lincoln himself never identified as an abolitionist. He did not believe strongly in the racial equality of blacks; his objections to slavery were grounded on the cruel and inhumane treatment of slaves. Like many famous politicians in American history who are known today for their anti-slavery views, Lincoln was committed to ending slavery legally and gradually. He supported the end of the slave trade in Washington D.C., and the graduated emancipation of American slaves over multiple generations. He also opposed the Dred Scott ruling, believing that black Americans were just as entitled as white Americans to the pursuit of "life, liberty, and the pursuit of happiness". But when the Whig party began to disintegrate in the 1850s, the agenda of the newly formed Republican party which took its place centered around opposition to slavery. Lincoln joined the Republican party in 1856, four years before he was elected the first Republican president.

Lincoln's presidency would have been impossible if not for a series of debates he participated in over the course of 1858. His debate opponent was Stephen A. Douglas, a fellow Illinoisan and one of the most prominent American politicians of the pre-Civil War period. Lincoln published a collection of the speeches he had delivered in opposition to Douglas, and the book, which became a best-seller, made Lincoln a household name and a figure of national significance. This new stature also made Lincoln a viable, if unexpected, front-runner for the nomination at the Republican National Convention of 1860—though it is generally agreed that he secured the nomination only because the delegates could not agree on any of the more likely nominees. Meanwhile, the Democratic party had also undergone a recent division, fielding two candidates, Stephen A. Douglas and John C. Breckinridge, against Lincoln during the 1860 presidential election. Lincoln won the electoral vote and carried all the northern states, while Breckinridge, who was from Kentucky, carried all the southern states, with the mid-Atlantic states falling to Douglas.

Prior to the election, South Carolina announced that it would secede from the Union if Lincoln should become president, and on December 20, 1860, secession was declared. Lincoln took office with the country already divided. Though Presidents Andrew Jackson and Zachary Taylor had both declared their willingness to send federal troops south to quell rebellion, neither had actually been required to do so. Lincoln waited until Confederate troops fired on Ft. Sumter on April 12, 1861, before formally acknowledging that a state of civil war existed in the United States. He called for 75,000 volunteers to fight for the preservation of the Union. The secession of Virginia, Arkansas, and Tennessee swiftly followed this announcement.

The first three years of the war went badly for the Union, and Lincoln's popularity suffered accordingly. He was frustrated by the insistence of Congressional Democrats that he arrive at a peace settlement with the Confederacy, and was equally frustrated by Union generals who were conducting the war at an unsatisfactorily slow pace. The senior officers of both the Union and Confederate armies had been trained at West Point according to traditional European rules of war, in which open battle was to be avoided as much as possible, emphasizing instead the capture of strategic locations and supply lines, such as the Confederate capitol city of Richmond, Virginia. Though Lincoln himself had little military experience, he educated himself on military strategy through intensive reading, and came to the conclusion that the only way to win a war against an enemy that was determined to fight to the death in order to preserve slavery was to destroy their armies. Lincoln removed one general after another from command of the Army of the Potomac, until the war record of an officer named Ulysses S. Grant was drawn to his attention. Grant had irritated his commanding officers several times by exceeding or ignoring orders to refrain from engaging the enemy in open battle. In March of 1864, Lincoln appointed Grant to take charge of the Union armies, over the direct objection of his cabinet members. Under Grant, and his close subordinate William Sherman, a policy of total war was adopted towards the Confederate south, hastening the war to its end, albeit at terrible cost to human life.

The first major Union victory of the war was the Battle of Antietam, fought in late 1862. In January of 1863, Lincoln announced the terms of the Emancipation Proclamation. It was a measure he had been considering since the beginning of the war, but Lincoln had chosen to wait until after the Union won a major battle before making the announcement, because he did not wish for it to appear that he was striking vengefully at the south out of frustration over Union losses. Lincoln had come to realize that the Confederacy would never surrender as long as they thought there was a hope of a victory or a peace agreement that would permit the institution of slavery to survive. The Emancipation Proclamation, though it did not free slaves throughout the Union, declared that any slave belonging to Confederates in rebellion against the Union were free and would be treated as such if they could escape to Union lines. It was a measure that struck at the heart of the Confederate cause, and one that undermined the confidence of the South's European allies, who had been considering the possibility of recognizing the legitimacy of the Confederate government.

When the Civil War began, most Americans, both in the north and in the south, believed that the war would end quickly, with only light casualties on either side. Instead, the war dragged on for years, saw unprecedented casualties, and devastated national morale. Lincoln, as president, naturally received the blame, and as the 1864 presidential election began to approach, Lincoln was forced to acknowledge that the likelihood of his being re-elected was small. He was facing criticism both from those who blamed him for not negotiating with the south, and from members of his own party who believed that he was not fighting hard enough to end slavery permanently. One of Lincoln's own generals, George McClellan, ran against Lincoln as the Democratic candidate during the 1864 election. However, Major General William Sherman captured the southern stronghold of Atlanta two months before the election, dealing a devastating blow to the Confederacy, and turning the tide of the war decisively in the Union's favor. Lincoln's popularity surged wildly, and he won re-election by a landslide.

In January of 1865, Congress passed the 13th Amendment to the Constitution, which declared slavery illegal throughout all of the United States, except as punishment for crime. Unlike the Emancipation Proclamation, the amendment prohibited slavery everywhere in the United States, including the four slave states, or border states, which had remained loyal to the Union. Radical Republicans—the abolitionist wing of the Republican party—had proposed similar bills in the past, to no effect. Lincoln recognized that so long as slavery existed anywhere in the U.S., the country would always be at risk of another civil war, and that the Confederate states would not surrender so long as they believed there was a chance of preserving slavery as an institution. By freeing all American slaves, the 13th Amendment left the south with little to fight for.

The Civil War came to an effective end on April 9, 1865, when Confederate general Robert E. Lee surrendered the Army of Northern Virginia to Ulysses S. Grant in Appomattox, Virginia. Lincoln immediately ordered his generals to allow all Southerners to return to their homes, keeping their personal possessions with them. He also expressed the hope that Confederate leaders such as President Jefferson Davis would go quietly abroad in order to avoid the necessity of a trial that would only rub salt in the wounds of defeat. With the rebellion crushed, Lincoln's chief concern was to see the country united once more.

Less than a week after Lee's surrender, Lincoln, his wife Mary, and another couple attended a performance of the play *Our American Cousin* at Ford's Theater in Washington. Ulysses and Julia Grant were also invited to attend, but backed out at the last moment. It was well known that

Lincoln's life might be in danger, as there had been several threats against him, and he had been warned to take special precautions the night of April 14th. During the play, an actor named John Wilkes Booth entered the president's box silently and fired a pistol at Lincoln, the bullet striking him in the back of the head. Lincoln was carried across the street where he was attended by army surgeons, but by the next morning, he was dead. Though he was not the first president to die in office, he was the first of four American presidents to date to be assassinated. Lincoln's body was returned for burial to Springfield, Illinois, and his coffin was displayed to mourners in every city it passed through. Since his death, Lincoln has been elevated to a status shared by no other American president save for George Washington; just as Washington is known as the father of his country, Lincoln is remembered as the savior of the union.

Memorable quote:

"I am naturally anti-slavery. If slavery is not wrong, nothing is wrong. I can not remember when I did not so think, and feel. And yet I have never understood that the Presidency conferred upon me an unrestricted right to act officially upon this judgment and feeling. It was in the oath I took that I would, to the best of my ability, preserve, protect, and defend the Constitution of the United States. I could not take the office without taking the oath. Nor was it my view that I might take an oath to get power, and break the oath in using the power. I understood, too, that in ordinary civil administration this oath even forbade me to practically indulge my primary abstract judgment on the moral question of slavery. I had publicly declared this many times, and in many ways. And I aver that, to this day, I have done no official act in mere deference to my abstract judgment and feeling on slavery. I did understand however, that my oath to preserve the constitution to the best of my ability, imposed upon me the duty of preserving, by every indispensable means, that government —

that nation — of which that constitution was the organic law."

--from a conversation between Abraham Lincoln and several Kentucky statesmen, later reported to Albert G. Hodges, 1864.

Seventeen

Andrew Johnson

(1808-1875)

Time in Office

(1865-1869)

Andrew Johnson was born on December 29, 1808, in Raleigh, North Carolina, to Jacob and Mary McDonough Johnson. Johnson's father died when he was three years old, leaving his mother to raise Andrew and his older brother William in straitened financial circumstances.

She earned a living as a seamstress and a laundress, even after her remarriage. When Andrew and William Johnson were old enough to learn a trade, their mother had them apprenticed to a local tailor named Selby. At Selby's shop, Johnson learned to read and write, and also gained exposure to important books and ideas of the day. Though Johnson and his brother were legally obligated to serve out their apprenticeship until they turned 21, they ran away after five years, prompting Selby to put out advertisements for their arrest and return for a reward of five dollars. After several years making a living as an itinerant tailor in small towns in North and South Carolina, Johnson returned to Raleigh in the hopes of coming to an arrangement with Selby, but was forced to leave the city to avoid arrest. The Johnson family later moved to Tennessee, where Johnson set up a successful tailoring business, with an income that permitted him to get married, in 1827, to Eliza McCardle. The justice of the peace who performed the ceremony was Mordecai Lincoln, who was a first cousin of Abraham Lincoln's father, Thomas. The couple would go on to have five children, including two daughters and three sons.

Like Selby's tailor shop, where men came daily to read to the tailors while they were working, Johnson's tailor shop became a sort of salon for the politically-minded men of Greeneville. Haunted by a strong sense of social inferiority due to his humble, log cabin origins, Johnson worked hard to supply the deficiencies of his education, and was encouraged in this by his wife. Johnson's politics were more or less aligned with those of the Democratic party. By the time of his election as a city alderman in 1829, Johnson's position on slavery had been cemented by the fallout of Nat Turner's rebellion, a short-lived slave uprising in which a small band of slaves murdered several white families before being arrested and executed. Johnson supported measures written into the new Tennessee state constitution which excluded free persons of color from being able to vote.

Johnson's political career began in 1835, after his election to the Tennessee state legislature. As a poor southerner, he advocated for the rights of poor whites on the western frontier, and for popular sovereignty of the individual states, though he was firmly against secession. In 1843, Johnson was elected to the U.S. House of Representatives, where he continued to support the institution of slavery, proclaiming it an indispensable part of the nation's heritage. Johnson served five terms in Congress, until the gains made by the Whig party in Tennessee made it impossible for him to be re-elected. In 1853, however, Johnson was elected governor of Tennessee, a position he fulfilled for two terms. Johnson found his tenure as governor frustrating, since he had no power to veto legislation, and could only support his agenda by giving advice to the legislature and by distributing key appointments to Democrats who supported him.

In 1856, Johnson once again turned his attention to national politics, and contemplated making a bid for his party's nomination for president. Realizing that he was too unknown outside of Tennessee to be successful, he instead set his sights on the U.S. Senate. He was elected, but his election met with harsh criticism from local newspapers and Tennessee Whigs, one of whom declared Johnson to be "the vilest radical and most unscrupulous demagogue in the Union." As a senator, Johnson aligned himself with other southern Democrats against the Homestead Act, which would have encouraged widespread settlement of the most remote areas of the western frontier. Democrats feared that the territories would never accept slavery, since the presence of wealthy white slave-owners made it impossible for poor white settlers to compete against cheap hired slave labor. Though Johnson remained steadfast in his support for slavery, he remained equally steadfast in his support for the integrity of the Union.

In 1860, the election of President Abraham Lincoln prompted the immediate secession of several southern states, including Tennessee. Johnson publicly denounced the secession, affirmed his loyalty to the Union, and became the only Senator from a southern state who continued to participate in the legitimate government of the United States during the war. Though Johnson's family was ostracized in Tennessee, Lincoln rewarded Johnson's loyalty by making him military governor of the state after it was taken back into Union hands. Johnson's relationship with Lincoln was uneasy throughout much of Lincoln's administration. He opposed the Emancipation Proclamation until it was made clear that slave states loyal to the Union—Tennessee counted, since it had been subdued and placed under Union government— would be exempted from its terms. In 1864, facing the likely prospect that he would not win a second election as president, Lincoln asked Johnson to become his running mate, hoping that Johnson's reputation as a southern slavery supporter would help sway more votes in his favor.

Shortly after Lincoln's second inaugural, he was assassinated by John Wilkes Booth. Unbeknownst to Johnson at the time, he was also one of the targets of Booth's expansive assassination plot, but the person assigned to carry out his murder never made his scheduled appearance. Johnson was sworn in as the 17th president of the United States in the early hours of April 15, 1865, three hours after Lincoln succumbed to his injuries.

Lincoln had seen the war to its end, but the monumental task of Reconstruction lay before his successor. Johnson was an unabashed white supremacist and it was left to him to integrate newly freed black Americans into society, both in the south and across the country. Radical Republicans in Congress were insistent that full suffrage must be granted to black Americans in order to guarantee their rights, but Johnson, who was president for eight months before Congress came back into session, used the powers of his office to settle the terms of Reconstruction to his own taste. Johnson issued a general pardon to any Confederate who was willing to swear allegiance to the Union, and he likewise pardoned Confederate vice-president Alexander Stephens, rather than charging him with treason. Johnson exerted no pressure on the southern states to enforce laws that would ensure the quality of free blacks. For decades after the war, there would be two sets of laws in the south, one for whites, and "black codes" for black southerners. When Congress came back into session, Johnson vetoed both the Freedmen's Bureau bill and the Civil Rights Act, though his vetoes were overturned. As a direct result, in June of 1866, Congress ratified the 14th Amendment, which explicitly disallows the president from removing high-ranking federal officials from office without the approval of the Senate.

Johnson, who at heart remained a populist, delivered a series of public speeches prior to the 1866 midterm elections, attempting to rally support for Democratic candidates who would support his own policies. His attempt to appeal directly to the American people failed, and Republicans swept Congress during the election. By 1867, Johnson, aware that his power was all but eroded, fired secretary of war and Lincoln appointee, Edwin Stanton, in direct violation of the 14th Amendment. In February of the following year, Johnson was impeached by the House of Representatives, though his impeachment was overturned in the Senate by a single vote.

Andrew Johnson lived another six years after completing Lincoln's second term of office. In 1874, he was elected to the Senate, where he opposed President Ulysses S. Grant's policies in the south. That summer, on July 31, 1875,

Johnson died of a stroke in Elizabethton, Tennessee, while visiting his daughters Mary and Martha. He was later buried near his adopted home of Greeneville. In accordance with his instructions, his body was shrouded in an American flag and his head pillowed on a copy of the Constitution.

Memorable quotes:

"I must be permitted to say that I have been almost overwhelmed by the announcement of the sad event which has so recently occurred. I feel incompetent to perform duties so important and responsible as those which have been so unexpectedly thrown upon me.

"The only assurance that I can now give of the future is reference to the past. The course which I have taken in the past in connection with this rebellion must be regarded as a guaranty of the future. My past public life, which has been long and laborious, has been founded, as I in good conscience believe, upon a great principle of right, which lies at the basis of all things. The best energies of my life have been spent in endeavoring to establish and perpetuate the principles of free government, and I believe that the Government in passing through its present perils will settle down upon principles consonant with popular rights more permanent and enduring than heretofore. I must be permitted to say, if I understand the feelings of my own heart, that I have long labored to ameliorate and elevate the condition of the great mass of the American people. Toil and an honest advocacy of the great principles of free government have been my lot. Duties have been mine; consequences are God's. This has been the foundation of my political creed, and I feel that in the end the Government will triumph and that these great principles will be permanently established."

--from Andrew Johnson's first address to his cabinet as President, 1865.

Part Five: The Gilded Age

Eighteen

Ulysses S. Grant

(1822-1885)

Time in Office

(1869-1877)

Hiram Ulysses Grant was born April 27, 1822, in
Point Pleasant, Ohio, to parents Jesse and
Hannah Simpson Grant, the oldest of the
couple's six children. Grant's ancestors
numbered amongst the Puritans who settled the
Massachusetts Bay Colony in the 1630s, and his
paternal grandfather fought in the Continental
Army during the Revolutionary War. Unusually
for American presidents of his era, Grant was not
considered a dedicated or especially promising
scholar as a boy, though he had access to formal

education throughout his childhood. Grant's specialty lay with animals. An uncommonly gifted horseman, he was handling the team that transported supplies to and from his father's farm before he was a teenager. Grant was not especially ambitious in his youth, but at his father's insistence he enrolled at West Point in 1839 and graduated 1843. At West Point, he was considered quiet and unwilling to draw attention to himself, preferring to read classic literature in his spare hours, though his extraordinary horsemanship drew the notice of his superiors. It was at West Point that Grant adopted the name "Ulysses S. Grant". Congressman Thomas L. Hamer, who sponsored Grant's application to the military academy at the request of Grant's father, had mistakenly put down "Ulysses" as Grant's first name on the official forms, and inserted "S" for his middle initial because it was the first letter of his mother's maiden name. According to West Point tradition, new cadets were given nicknames which followed them throughout their military career; Grant was nicknamed

"Sam" due to the fact that the initials "U.S." suggested the iconic figure of "Uncle Sam" to Grant's classmates. Friends continued to refer to Grant as Sam throughout his life.

Grant did not initially intend to pursue a career in the military. Having ranked 21st out of 39 members of his graduating class, he did not seem to be marked out for military greatness. Grant's goal was to become a mathematics instructor in a private school after his years of obligatory post-graduation military service were fulfilled. The Mexican-American War altered his plans, however, as did his marriage to Julia Dent, sister of a West Point classmate. Grant fought under the general command of General Zachary Taylor, whose pragmatic command style made a deeply favorable impression on the young officer. Soldiers who had served under Taylor and would later serve under Grant observed a number of similarities between their command styles. Grant did not stand upon the formalities or privileges that divided officers from enlisted soldiers. Even as a general, he tended to dress in a mixture of a private's uniform and civilian clothing, unless the occasion demanded formality.

After the war's end, Grant, who had received several brevet promotions, was formally elevated to the rank of captain, after which he was posted to stations in the Pacific northwest. His wife Julia, who was pregnant at the time of his posting, remained with family in St. Louis, and the separation depressed Grant deeply. In July of 1854, Grant abruptly resigned his army commission, for reasons which are still disputed by historians. It is generally agreed that Grant was forced to resign by a superior who believed he was neglecting his duties because of drunkenness, but the reputation which followed Grant afterwards for being a heavy drinker may have been based on nothing more than rumor. After leaving the northwest, Grant returned to his family and attempted to operate a farm for several years, only to meet with a series of misfortunes that devastated him financially.

During this period of his life, Grant owned his first and only slave, a man named William Jones, who was given to Grant as a gift by his father-in-law. Within a year, Grant had Jones emancipated, though the cash from his sale would have relieved him of his debts.

As soon as President Abraham Lincoln announced that he was seeking volunteers to quell the rebellion in the south, Grant, then living in Galena, Illinois, looked for an opportunity to put his military experience to use in the service of his country. He had difficulty obtaining a commission at first because he refused to vie with other former officers for prestigious positions. Eventually, Grant came to the notice of Congressman Elihu B. Washburne, who would advocate for Grant throughout the course of the war and eventually bring him to the attention of Lincoln. On June 17, 1861, Grant was made colonel of the 21st Illinois Regiment; a month later, he received a promotion to brigadier general.

Grant spent the war in the western theater, where he won a series of victories for the Union, often by acting against or ignoring the orders of his battle-shy superiors. After Grant's first major victory at Ft. Donelson, the Confederate commander, who had been a friend of Grant's at West Point, asked for a meeting to discuss the terms of surrender. Departing from the antiquated, chivalric battlefield code that was taught at West Point, Grant replied, "No terms except immediate and unconditional surrender." When news of the incident made the papers, Grant became famous for a new nickname: "Unconditional Surrender" Grant. Other major victories attributed to Grant prior to his assuming supreme control of the Union army include the battles of Shiloh and Vicksburg, the latter of which is credited with turning the tide of the war definitively in the Union's favor.

Lincoln's decision to place Grant in supreme command of the Union armies stemmed from the fact that his more senior generals persisted in avoiding open battle whenever possible, whereas Grant, realizing that the Confederacy would never surrender until their army was destroyed and it was impossible for them to fight any longer, determinedly pursued battle with the enemy even when ordered to do the opposite. Told that Grant was an unreliable drunkard, Lincoln asked his war secretary to find out what Grant's preferred drink was, because he wanted to send a case of it to each of his generals. When Lincoln's cabinet recommended that he fire Grant, he famously replied, "I can't spare this man. He fights." Grant was promoted to the rank of lieutenant general—a rank wielded by no other American officer since George Washington—and given charge of the Union army in March of 1864. Grant promptly began to organize a two-pronged push into the heart of the Confederacy, with William T. Sherman as his deputy. Sherman's task was to capture Atlanta and destroy the southern armies in the southern states, while Grant pursued pursued Robert E. Lee and the Army of Northern Virginia in the

Battle of the Wilderness, finally forcing Lee's surrender in April of 1865.

Grant was immediately invited to Washington D.C. to meet President Lincoln and receive congratulations from a grateful American public. During this visit, Grant and his wife Julia were invited to accompany President Lincoln and his wife to Ford's Theater to view a performance of a play called *Our American Cousin*. The Grants declined the invitation because Julia Grant had taken a strong disliking to Mary Todd Lincoln's company and did not wish to spend the evening with her. Lincoln was assassinated during the course of the play, and Grant was immediately summoned by the war office to return to Washington. He was devastated by Lincoln's death, and for the rest of his life regretted his absence from the theater that night, as he was convinced that he could have overpowered Booth and possibly saved Lincoln's life.

Grant was elected president in 1868, the most popular and highly sought-after presidential candidate since George Washington. Both parties invited him to run on their ballot. Yet compared to his role in winning the Civil War, Grant's presidency is often considered a disappointing and unremarkable footnote to his career. Despite his first administration being plagued by scandal, he was re-elected in 1872, only to face the Panic of 1873, one of the most severe recessions in American history. Even with these failures behind him, he was nominated for a third term in the election of 1880, though he did not become the party's candidate. After his administration ended, Grant and his family toured Europe, to much acclaim and celebration. As had happened during the years between Grant resigning his first commission and re-entering the army after the outbreak of the Civil War, Grant faced severe financial difficulty when he returned to private life. His son, Ulysses Jr., called Buck, was defrauded by a business associate, who vanished with a large sum of money that Buck had borrowed from his father; Grant lost $100,000 of his own money, and was in debt for another $150,000 he had raised on Buck's behalf. The Grant family was forced to sell all their properties and most of their valuable possessions in order to pay the loan back. Not until Grant began writing his memoirs of the war was he able to make enough money to provide his family with a comfortable living. In 1884, Grant was diagnosed with cancer of the tongue, and though he lived long enough to finish writing his memoirs, he died before they were published. The money they earned, however, provided for Julia and their children for the rest of their lives. Grant died on July 23, 1885, and was given a state funeral, with mourning observed across the United States.

Memorable quote:

"Our liberties remain unimpaired; the bondmen have been freed from slavery; we have become possessed of the respect, if not the friendship, of all civilized nations. Our progress has been great in all the arts—in science, agriculture, commerce, navigation, mining, mechanics, law, medicine, etc.; and in general education the progress is likewise encouraging. Our thirteen States have become thirty-eight, including Colorado (which has taken the initiatory steps to become a State), and eight Territories, including the Indian Territory and Alaska, and excluding Colorado, making a territory extending from the Atlantic to the Pacific. On the south we have extended to the Gulf of Mexico, and in the west from the Mississippi to the Pacific.

"As the primary step, therefore, to our advancement in all that has marked our progress in the past century, I suggest for your earnest consideration, and most earnestly recommend it, that a constitutional amendment be submitted to the legislatures of the several States for ratification, making it the duty of each of the several States to establish and forever maintain free public schools adequate to the education of all the children in the rudimentary branches within their respective limits, irrespective of sex, color, birthplace, or religions; forbidding the teaching in said schools of religious, atheistic, or pagan tenets; and prohibiting the granting of any school funds or school taxes, or any part thereof, either by legislative, municipal, or other authority, for the benefit or in aid, directly or indirectly, of any religious sect or denomination, or in aid or for the benefit of any other object of any nature or kind whatever."

--from Ulysses Grant's seventh State of the Union address, 1875.

Nineteen

Rutherford B. Hayes

(1822-1893)

Time in Office

(1877-1881)

Rutherford B. Hayes was born in Delware, Ohio, to Sophia Birchard Hayes, a widow. Hayes's father, Rutherford Hayes, Jr., a farmer of modest means, died approximately three months before his son's birth. The couple had one other child, a daughter named Fanny, who was two years Hayes's senior. After their fathers' death, Hayes and his sister were raised by their mother and their maternal uncle, Sardis Birchard, who was a businessman of standing in his community. When Hayes was a young child, the family moved from Delaware to the town of Lower Sandusky (the present day city of Fremont), also in Ohio. Like many presidents before him, Hayes was descended from English colonists who settled in North America in the early 17th century.

Hayes had access to regular schooling as a child, and began attending the Methodist Norwalk Seminary in Norwalk, Ohio, when he was fourteen years old, later transferring to The Webb School in Connecticut, where he began studying Latin and Greek. In 1842, at the age of 20, Hayes graduated from Kenyon College, making him the first president to matriculate at a western university. In 1845, he received a law degree from Harvard. Though the majority of all presidents who preceded him also studied law, Hayes was the first to obtain a degree from a law school. He was admitted to the bar in Ohio immediately after his graduation and began practicing law in Cincinnati. As a lifelong opponent of slavery, Hayes was one of the earliest members of the Republic Party, formed after the dissolution of the Whig Party on a strong anti-slavery platform.

In 1852, Hayes was married to Lucy Webb, who was one of the earliest graduates of Wesleyan Women's College. Lucy Webb Hayes would become the first First Lady in American history who possessed a university education. The marriage produced eight children, only five of whom survived to adulthood. Prior to the Civil War, Hayes was active in local politics, and in

1858 he was appointed city solicitor (a position similar to attorney general) for the town of Cincinnati. Upon the outbreak of war in 1861, however, Hayes immediately sought a military commission in the Union army. He was given the rank of major and placed in charge of the 23rd Ohio Regiment. After being injured in battle, he was given a brevet promotion to major general. He was still in the midst of the fighting when he received word that he had received his party's nomination for the 1864 Congressional election, and though he accepted the nomination, he refused to divert his attention from the war in order to campaign on his own behalf, remarking that, "An officer fit for duty who at this crisis would abandon his post to electioneer for a seat in Congress ought to be scalped."

When the Civil War ended in 1865, Hayes resigned his commission and began his first term in the U.S. House of Representatives. He served two terms in the House before resigning in 1867 in order to be eligible for the upcoming gubernatorial race. Hayes was elected governor of Ohio twice. At the conclusion of his second term in 1872, he was ready to return to private life, and after an unsuccessful bid for Congress in 1872, he returned his energies and attentions to his legal practice. In 1875, however, the Ohio Republican Party asked him to run for governor once again, and his election made him the first governor in the history of Ohio to serve for three terms. As a faithful party member, Hayes ran on a platform that included voting enfranchisement for black Americans, as well as strengthening the national currency with a gold standard backing.

The presidential election of 1876 saw division in the ranks of the Republican party. A number of Republicans supported the re-election of President Ulysses Grant to an unprecedented third term in office. The remaining party members were divided in their support of two different candidates. One faction backed James G. Blaine of Maine, who was then Speaker of the House. Hayes was the third contender. In a manner similar to how Abraham Lincoln secured the Republican nomination in 1860, Hayes emerged as the "compromise candidate"; Grant's supporters would not back Blaine, Blaine's supporters would not back Grant, but enough of Grant and Blaine's advocates were willing to support Hayes to make him the leading candidate by default.

As President Grant's administration had been plagued by implications of scandal and corruption, Hayes's reputation for loyalty and meticulous honesty seemed to offer the chance of a fresh start in the world of Washington politics. Hayes's opponent in the national election was New York governor Samuel J. Tilden, who was similar to Hayes in several respects, as he also had a reputation for honesty and fair dealing, and he supported the same hard currency measures that Hayes did. With the Civil War still fresh in recent memory, many people were reluctant to see a Democrat in the White House. Tilden appeared, at first, to have won the election. But a special election commission was required to sort through the ballots after three southern states, Florida, Louisiana, and South Carolina, each returned two different election counts—one tallied by the Democratic party, one tallied by the states' Republicans. The 15-person commission, which was comprised chiefly of Republicans, made their investigation and determined that the disputed electoral votes rightly belonged to Hayes. In order to persuade Democrats in the south to accept the commission's findings, Congressional Republicans had to agree to the removal of the federal troops stationed in the southern states to enforce Reconstruction-era laws meant to safeguard black Americans.

On March 3, 1877, one day after the election was finally decided in Hayes's favor, he took the oath of office privately; two days later, a formal inauguration took place. Despite the concessions made to the Democrats, many remained bitter about Hayes's election, regarding it as having been stolen from Tilden by the Republican election commissioners. The election of Rutherford B. Hayes effectively saw the end of Reconstruction efforts in the south. The federal officers who had been overseeing the reforms were replaced by influential white Southerners, who were given thousands of dollars in funds in order to improve infrastructure, such as rebuilding railway lines that had been destroyed by Union troops during the war. This mollified southern Democrats somewhat, but also had the effect of alienating some of Hayes's Republican supporters.

During Hayes's administration, anti-corruption was the focus, with a particular emphasis on ending the patronage system by which high level government appointments were assigned to the friends and associates of the person with the power to make the appointments. Hayes wished to institute civil service reforms that would ensure all government appointments were made on the basis of merit alone. This brought him into conflict with powerful New York senator Roscoe Conkling, after Hayes asked for the resignation of future president Chester Arthur, who occupied a high position in the New York customs house. Hayes had no complaints about Arthur's execution of his duties, but his was a patronage appointment enabled by Conkling, and Hayes felt that he should resign as a matter of principle. Hayes faced other domestic policy issues as well, including a weak economy that was still recovering from the Civil War. Two members of Congress, in an effort to bolster the flagging economy, proposed a bill (the Bland-Allison Act) which struck at the heart of Hayes's hard currency platform by proposing that the government begin minting coins in silver rather than gold. Hayes vetoed the Bland-Allison Act, but the bill passed both of houses of Congress despite his opposition.

In 1881, in keeping with the pledge made in his inaugural address, Hayes chose not to run for re-election. He and his family left Washington to return to Ohio, where their estate, Spiegel Grove, awaited them. Hayes lived for twelve years after the end of his presidency, and he devoted his time to supporting humanitarian and philanthropic endeavors, such as prison reform, and educational endowments to provide free public schooling for children. Hayes became a trustee on the boards of Ohio Wesleyan, Ohio State, and Western Reserve Universities, and in 1882, became the president of the John F. Slater Education Fund for Freedmen, which provided money for the education of black American men. Famed sociologist W.E.B. DuBois was among the beneficiaries of the trust.

Rutherford B. Hayes died of heart failure on January 17, 1893, in the company of two of his children. He was seventy years old. His wife Lucy had predeceased him some three years earlier, and the two were buried together in Fremont, Ohio.

Memorable quote:

"One of its [James A. Garfield's assassination] lessons, perhaps its most important lesson, is the folly, the wickedness, and the danger of the extreme and bitter partisanship which so largely prevails in our country. This partisan bitterness is greatly aggravated by that system of appointments and removals which deals with public offices as rewards for services rendered to political parties or to party leaders. Hence crowds of importunate place-hunters of whose dregs Guiteau is the type. The required reform [of the civil service] will be accomplished whenever the people imperatively demand it, not only of their Executive, but also of their legislative officers. With it, the class to which the assassin belongs will lose their occupation, and the temptation to try "to administer government by assassination" will be taken away."

--letter from Rutherford B. Hayes to Emile Kahn upon the assassination of President James Garfield, 1881.

Twenty

James A. Garfield

(1831-1881)

Time in Office

(March 4, 1881-September 19, 1881)

James Abram Garfield was born on November 19, 1831, in Orange Township, Ohio, the youngest of the five children of Abram and Eliza Garfield. As was often the custom in an age of high infant mortality rates, Garfield was name for an elder brother who had died before he was born. Abram Garfield, a wrestler, died when Garfield was two years old, leaving his family mired in poverty. Eliza Garfield became an active member of the Church of Christ, but otherwise lacked much support from her community, especially after her second marriage in 1842 ended in a bitter divorce eight years later.

Without access to schools or formal education as a young boy, Garfield voraciously read any books he could acquire. At the age of sixteen, Garfield left home to seek employment on a canal boat, but after illness forced him to return home after six months, he was offered a place at Geauga Seminary, which he attended between 1848 and 1850. Garfield was a gifted pupil who excelled in languages and public speaking. In 1851, at the age of twenty, he began attending the Western Reserve Eclectic Institute, and later Williams College in Massachusetts, where he graduated as salutatorian. Having been hired as a part time instructor at the college while he was still a student, Garfield decided to become a school teacher, though he disliked "seeking places", or job hunting, which teachers on yearly contracts had to do often. Public speaking became a hobby in his spare time, and the devoutly religious Garfield remonstrated against slavery and spoke in support of the Republican Party. Having returned to Ohio after taking a degree at a prestigious east coast university, he found himself a figure of some importance in his hometown. In 1858, Garfield was married to Lucretia Randolph, who had been a fellow student of his at both Geauga Seminary and Western Reserve Eclectic Institute; the couple would go on to have seven children.

The following year, 1859, Garfield embarked on his political career. While studying law, he was elected to the Ohio legislature, where he would serve until 1861. The outbreak of the Civil War coincided with the end of his term of office, and Garfield promptly joined the Union army, receiving a commission as a lieutenant colonel, though he was promoted to brigadier general the following year. In 1862, the same year he led a brigade during the Battle of Shiloh, Garfield was elected to the U.S. Congress, though Congress would not resume session until 1863, giving him the opportunity to finish out his military service. Once ensconced in Washington, he gained an important patron and ally in Abraham Lincoln's treasury secretary, Salmon P. Chase, who was the leader of the Radical Republican, or abolitionist, faction of Congress. Garfield himself became a member of the Radical Republicans, and like other hardline abolitionists of the era, often grew frustrated with Lincoln's seeming unwillingness to take swift, decisive action to end slavery once and for all. Unlike Lincoln, who was determined to see slavery ended by legal means, Garfield did not believe that Confederate slave-owners were entitled to Constitutional protections against seizure of private property, and believed that plantations and slaves alike should be seized by the legitimate government of the United States where possible.

After the end of the war and the assassination of Abraham Lincoln, Garfield swung even further to the left, politically, after President Andrew Johnson gutted Reconstruction forms such as the Freedman's Bureau. He was among the majority of Congress who voted for Johnson to be impeached for violating the 14th Amendment. Garfield was nominated by the Republican Party during the 1880 election as a compromise candidate, like Hayes and Lincoln before him; his running mate, appointed by the convention, was Chester A. Arthur, who was far more moderate than the Radical Republicans.

Garfield's presidency lasted for only six months. During his brief administration, he continued many of Hayes's civil service reforms, re-organized the U.S. Post Office, championed free universal education, and appointed black Americans, such as Frederick Douglass, writer, orator, and former slave, to high government offices. On July 2, 1881, a low-level political speechmaker named Charles J. Guiteau, embittered by the fact that he had not received what he considered to be a just reward for his efforts to get Garfield elected, shot Garfield at the Baltimore and Potomac Railroad Station in Washington, D.C., just as Garfield was preparing to travel to New Jersey to spend the hot summer months in cooler climates. He was shot twice, once in the arm, and once in the back. It was the second bullet, which lodged in his abdomen, that proved fatal. Unlike Lincoln, who died within hours of being shot in the head by John Wilkes Booth, Garfield survived for two and a half months before succumbing to infection. His assassination came as a profound shock to the country; Lincoln's assassination, though it had catapulted the nation into chaos, was seen as an unrepeatable event, made possible only by the brutality of the war. No new provisions were made for the personal protection of the president after Lincoln's assassination, and no bodyguards had accompanied Garfield on the train platform at the time he was shot. One of the witnesses to the assassination was Garfield's secretary of war, Robert Todd Lincoln, Abraham Lincoln's oldest and only surviving son. Guiteau was convicted of the assassination and executed in 1882. Garfield's remains were returned to Ohio for burial.

Memorable quote:

"And first, we must recognize in all our action the stupendous facts of the war. In the very crisis of our fate God brought us face to face with the alarming truth that we must lose our own freedom or grant it to the slave. In the extremity of our distress we called upon the black man to help us save the Republic, and amid the very thunder of battle we made a covenant with him, sealed both with his blood and ours, and witnessed by Jehovah, that when the nation was redeemed he should be free and share with us the glories and blessings of freedom. In the solemn words of the great proclamation of emancipation, we not only declared the slaves forever free, but we pledged the faith of the nation 'to maintain their freedom', mark the words, ;to maintain their freedom'. The omniscient witness will appear in judgment against us if we do not fulfill that covenant. Have we done it? Have we given freedom to the black man? What is freedom? Is it a mere negation, the bare privilege of not being chained, bought and sold, branded and scourged? If this be all, then freedom is a bitter mockery, a cruel delusion, and it may well be questioned whether slavery were not better.

"But liberty is no negation. It is a substantive, tangible reality. It is the realization of those imperishable truths of the Declaration 'that all men are created equal', that the sanction of all just government is 'the consent of the governed'. Can these truths be realized until each man has a right be to heard on all matters relating to himself?"

--from an address by James Garfield to the U.S. House of Representatives, 1866.

Twenty-One

Chester A. Arthur

(1829-1886)

Time in Office

(1881-1885)

Chester Alan Arthur was born on October 5, 1829, in Fairfield, Vermont, to William Arthur, a schoolteacher and Baptist minister, and his wife Malvina Stone Arthur. The couple had met and married while William Arthur was working in Canada, near the Vermont border, and the family moved to Canada shortly after the birth of their first child. Chester Arthur was the fifth of their nine children, seven of whom lived to adulthood. When Arthur was a boy, his family moved frequently, often due to his father's strict abolitionist beliefs, which sometimes put him at odds with his congregation. Arthur had access to formal schooling as a boy, though he never remained at one school for long due, to the peripatetic nature of his father's profession.

Even as a child, Arthur took a precocious interest in political affairs. He first claimed loyalty to the Whig party as a school boy, idolizing famous Whig statesman Henry Clay, and defending Clay's reputation in a schoolyard brawl with other boys who professed similar loyalties to James K. Polk. At the age of sixteen, Arthur began attending Union College, in Schenectady, New York, where he studied the traditional classics-based curriculum. After graduating in 1848, Arthur made a living as a school teacher while studying at the State and National Law School in Ballston Spa, New York. For the next few years, he worked exclusively in education, becoming a school principal in several different districts. In 1854, he received his license to practice law in New York, and began developing a reputation as a young lawyer who was willing to represent black Americans who had been denied civil rights. In 1855, he represented a woman named Elizabeth Jennings Graham, who had been forced out of a streetcar full of white passengers, and the case helped lead to the desegregation of New York's public transportation system. By this time, Arthur was a member of the new Republican Party, attracted to its strong anti-slavery platform.

In 1859, after a courtship of three years, Arthur was married to Ellen Lewis Herndon, whose father was an officer in the U.S. navy. Only two of their children, a son and a daughter, survived to adulthood. Ellen Arthur would die of pneumonia prior to Arthur's election as president, and many of the social duties of the First Lady were fulfilled by Arthur's sister, Mary McElroy, during his administration. A year after Arthur's marriage, the Civil War broke out. Arthur volunteered for service in the Union army, and was made a quartermaster, in charge of gathering and distributing supplies to Union soldiers.

Chester Arthur was the fourth vice-president of the United States who attained presidential office due to the unexpected death of the previous occupant, and the second to do so because the previous president was assassinated. During the Republican National Convention of 1880, a closely debated contest between President Ulysses Grant, James Blaine, and

James Garfield, the nomination was given to Garfield, with Arthur as his running mate. Less than four months after Garfield's election, he was shot by Charles Guiteau; two and a half months later, Garfield was dead. Chester Arthur, who was in New York at the time, was informed of Arthur's death by a reporter. He was sworn into office shortly afterwards, at his Manhattan residence, by John R. Brady of the New York Supreme Court. Before setting out for New York, Arthur requested a special convening of the Senate, as a precaution to preserve the government: should anything happen to Arthur during the journey from New York to Washington, the Senate would then be in session, and thus empowered to elect a new Senate pro tempore, the government official who comes after the vice president in the Constitutional line of presidential succession.

During Arthur's administration, he emulated the example of Garfield and Hayes before him by supporting civil service reform, even though

Arthur himself had risen through the ranks of his party due in no small part to the partisanship system. Arthur signed the Pendleton Civil Service Act into law in 1883, mandating merit-based appointments to high level government positions, and prohibiting civil servants from being fired on an arbitrary political basis, or from being required to make financial donations to political campaigns. The Pendleton Act also created the Civil Service Commission, which was charged with enforcing the new law. Arthur also vetoed a bill which aimed to block all persons from China from immigrating to the United States for a period of ten years, but his veto was overridden by Congress. Arthur distinguished himself as being the first fashionable president since George Washington began receiving visitors to the Executive Mansion wearing a black velvet suit and a ceremonial sword at his hip. Nicknamed "Elegant Arthur", he owned a substantial wardrobe.

In 1882, Chester Arthur was diagnosed with a degenerative kidney disorder called Bright's disease. His health worsened steadily during the last years of his administration, and in 1884 he chose not to seek re-election. After leaving the White House, Arthur spent the remaining two years of his life in New York, where he practiced law until his health no longer permitted him to keep up with business. He died at home in Manhattan on November 18, 1886, and was buried next to his wife in Menands, New York.

Memorable quote:

"For the fourth time in the history of the Republic its Chief Magistrate has been removed by death. All hearts are filled with grief and horror at the hideous crime which has darkened our land, and the memory of the murdered President, his protracted sufferings, his unyielding fortitude, the example and achievements of his life, and the pathos of his death will forever illumine the pages of our history.

"For the fourth time the officer elected by the people and ordained by the Constitution to fill a vacancy so created is called to assume the Executive chair. The wisdom of our fathers, foreseeing even the most dire possibilities, made sure that the Government should never be imperiled because of the uncertainty of human life. Men may die, but the fabrics of our free institutions remain unshaken. No higher or more assuring proof could exist of the strength and permanence of popular government than the fact that though the chosen of the people be struck down his constitutional successor is peacefully installed without shock or strain except the sorrow which mourns the bereavement. All the noble aspirations of my lamented predecessor which found expression in his life, the measures devised and suggested during his brief Administration to correct abuses, to enforce economy, to advance prosperity, and to promote the general welfare, to Insure domestic security and maintain friendly and honorable relations with the nations of the earth, will be garnered in the hearts of the people; and it will be my earnest endeavor to profit, and to see that the nation shall profit, by his example and experience.

"Prosperity blesses our country. Our fiscal policy is fixed by law, is well grounded and generally approved. No threatening issue mars our foreign intercourse, and the wisdom, integrity, and thrift of our people may be trusted to continue undisturbed the present assured career of peace, tranquilly, and welfare. The gloom and anxiety which have enshrouded the country must make repose especially welcome now. No demand for speedy legislation has been heard; no adequate occasion is apparent for an unusual session of Congress. The Constitution defines the functions and powers of the executive as clearly as those of either of the other two departments of the Government, and he must answer for the just exercise of the discretion it permits and the performance of the duties it imposes. Summoned to these high duties and responsibilities and profoundly conscious of their magnitude and gravity, I assume the trust imposed by the Constitution, relying for aid on divine guidance and the virtue, patriotism, and intelligence of the American people."

--Chester Arthur's Address Upon Assuming the Office of the President of the United States, 1881.

Twenty-Two and Twenty-Four

Grover Cleveland

(1837-1908)

Time in Office

(1885-1889)

(1893-1897)

Stephen Grover Cleveland, the only president in American history to be elected to two non-consecutive terms, was born on March 18, 1837, in Caldwell, New Jersey, the fifth of the nine children of Presbyterian clergyman Richard Cleveland and his wife, Anne Neal Cleveland. Cleveland was descended from early American settlers, and the city of Cleveland, Ohio was named for one of his distant relatives. Cleveland's family moved to Fayetteville, New York in 1841, and most of his childhood was spent there. He attended the Fayetteville Academy and Clinton Liberal Academy until his father's death in 1853, when he began working as a school teacher in order to assist his mother financially. After his brother William began working for the New York Institute for the Blind, he assisted Cleveland in obtaining a position there. In 1854, an elder at his father's church offered to support Cleveland at university, provided he trained to become a minister. Cleveland declined the offer, and moved to Buffalo, New York, where he began working as a legal clerk for his uncle, Lewis Allen. By 1859, Cleveland was sufficiently well read in the law to be admitted to the New York bar. In 1862, he started a law practice of his own. The next year, with the Civil War underway, he exercised an option legally available to well-to-do men by paying for a substitute to take his place in the army, rather than fighting himself. His mother and younger sisters were almost entirely dependent on Cleveland's income, and Cleveland himself lived austerely, in a boarding house, in order to save money for them.

Cleveland's political career began in 1871, when he was elected sheriff of Eerie County in New York, though he served only two years before returning to the practice of law. In 1882, he was elected mayor of Buffalo, on an anti-corruption platform. From that point forward, his reputation and importance in the Democratic party assumed new proportions, and no sooner had he been elected mayor of Buffalo than he was asked to run for governor of New York, a position he assumed in 1883.

As president, Cleveland would become known for his record-breaking number of vetoes, but it was a habit which began during his gubernatorial career. Cleveland was an early deficit hawk, deeply opposed to any government spending he did not deem strictly necessary. This position endeared him to the voting public but alienated other members of the Democratic party, particularly in New York, where corruption was notoriously rampant.

Cleveland became the 22nd president of the United States in 1885, and the first Democrat elected since the Civil War, after a contentious and bitterly divisive race against Republican senator James G. Blaine. Scandal hounded both candidates, as it was revealed that Blaine had been involved in financial improprieties, and that Cleveland had been implicated in a paternity case with a woman to whom he was not married some ten years earlier. Despite opposition from powerful New York Democrats, Cleveland was elected due to the support of a Republican faction called the Mugwumps, who did not support their own party's candidate. During his first administration, Cleveland continued the trend of the last decade by fighting for civil service reform, and continued to take a dim view of government spending, setting the record for the most vetoes of any American president to that point. When Cleveland had been president for one year, he was married to Frances Folsom, a 21-year old college student from New York who was almost three decades Cleveland's junior. Though John Tyler was the first president to marry while in office, Cleveland was the first president to be married in the White House, and Frances Cleveland became the youngest First Lady in American history. Their marriage produced five children.

Though Cleveland ran for re-election in 1888, he was defeated by Benjamin Harrison, due to popular backlash against Cleveland's stance on low tariffs on foreign imports, which cost many working-class Americans their jobs. After leaving the White House, Cleveland returned to New York and began practicing law again.

In 1892, President Benjamin Harrison ran for re-election, but due to his wife's terminal illness, he did not take an active part in the campaign. Cleveland, who had received the Democratic nomination, likewise did not campaign on his own behalf, and the tone of the race was far different from the embittering conflict of the 1884 election. Though the New York political establishment had refused to support Cleveland during his first campaign, they backed him in the 1892 election. This second election victory, in which Cleveland carried a decisive majority of the electoral college, made Cleveland the 24th, as well as the 22nd, president of the United States.

During Cleveland's second administration, the Panic of 1893 struck the country's financial infrastructure, developing into the worst recession in American history to that time. At least 19% of Americans were unemployed, major railroads went bankrupt, banks failed, and the stock market crashed. The situation did not improve for three years, when the gold rush in the Canadian Yukon territory began, inciting a new generation of westward expansion and investment. Cleveland faced criticism for his handling of the social problems triggered by the crisis, such as his use of federal troops to break strikes against the railroads.

Despite his historic non-consecutive second term as president, Cleveland's popularity had flagged significantly by the time of the election of 1896. Though some members of the Democratic party supported Cleveland for a third term, he chose instead to support Congressman William Jennings Bryan for the Democratic nomination. Bryan, however, was defeated by Republican governor William McKinley. Cleveland lived another twelve years after leaving the White House the second time, retiring to Princeton, New Jersey, where he led a quiet life with his family, and served as a trustee of Princeton University. On June 24, 1908, when he was 71 years old, Cleveland died of a heart attack. He was buried in Princeton, near Nassau

Presbyterian Church. According to multiple witnesses, the last words Cleveland spoke on his deathbed were, "I have tried so hard to do right."

Memorable quote:

"It has been the boast of our government that it seeks to do justice in all things without regard to the strength or weakness of those with whom it deals. I mistake the American people if they favor the odious doctrine that there is no such thing as international morality; that there is one law for a strong nation and another for a weak one, and that even by indirection a strong power may with impunity despoil a weak one of its territory.

"By an act of war, committed with the participation of a diplomatic representative of the United States and without authority of Congress, the government of a feeble but friendly and confiding people has been overthrown. A substantial wrong has thus been done which a due regard for our national character as well as the rights of the injured people requires we should endeavor to repair. The Provisional Government has not assumed a republican or other constitutional form, but has remained a mere executive council or oligarchy, set up without the assent of the people. It has not sought to find a permanent basis of popular support and has given no evidence of an intention to do so. Indeed, the representatives of that government assert that the people of Hawaii are unfit for popular government and frankly avow that they can be best ruled by arbitrary or despotic power."

--from Grover Cleveland's message to Congress regarding the failed attempt to admit Hawaii to the Union, 1893.

Twenty-Three

Benjamin Harrison

(1833-1901)

Time in Office

(1889-1893)

Benjamin Harrison, grandson of the 9th American president, William Henry Harrison, was born on August 20, 1833, on his family's farm in North Bend, Ohio. He was the second of the eight children born to John Scott Harrison, a farmer and two-term Congressman, and Elizabeth Ramsey, his wife. Harrison's election made him the second dynastic president in American history. William Henry Harrison was elected president when Benjamin was seven years old, though he was not present for the inauguration.

Harrison was educated privately by tutors as a boy, after which he enrolled in Farmer's College near Cincinnati for two years when he was fourteen. In 1850, Harrison began attending Miami University in Oxford, Ohio, where he graduated in 1852. A year later, he married Caroline Lavinia Scott, the daughter of a faculty member at Farmer's College. They would have two children, a son, Russell, and a daughter, Mary. Harrison studied law for a time under

Judge Bellamy Storer of Cincinnati, and was admitted to the bar in Ohio in 1854. Shortly afterwards, Harrison used a small inheritance to move himself and his family to Indianapolis, Indiana, where he began practicing law.

Inspired by the example of his father and grandfather, Harrison took an early interest in a political career, to the approval of his wife and the disapproval of his father, who believed that Harrison would find politics distasteful. Harrison devoted his early career to Indiana state politics, and became an early member of the newly formed Republican Party, due to his strong opposition to slavery expansion. When the Civil War began in 1861, Harrison sought and received a lieutenant's commission in the Union Army, commanding the 70th Indiana Volunteer Infantry Regiment. By 1865, he had received a brevet promotion to brigadier general; Harrison would be the last high ranking officer from the Civil War era to become president. At the war's conclusion, Harrison return to Indiana to practice law. In 1872 and 1876, he made a bid for office in the Indiana gubernatorial elections. He failed to gain the Republican nomination in 1872, and though he received the nomination in 1876, he was narrowly defeated by the Democratic candidate.

Harrison was elected to the U.S. Senate in 1881, where he served until 1887. During his senatorial career he became known for championing the rights of Native Americans, frontier settlers, and Civil War veterans who depended on government pensions. He took a principled stand, citing his religious convictions, against other members of his own party when he opposed the Chinese Exclusion Act of 1882, which placed a ten year hold on any Chinese immigration to the United States. In 1887, Harrison lost his bid for re-election to the Senate, but in 1888, he received the Republican nomination, becoming the party's presidential candidate. Harrison's opponent was President Grover Cleveland, who would also be his successor. Harrison's victory over Cleveland was controversial, because he lost the popular vote by a count of 90,000, but carried 233 electoral votes to Cleveland's 168.

Harrison differed sharply in his policies from Cleveland, whose strong opposition to protective tariffs led to a financial crisis during his second term. Harrison was a proponent of tariffs and of expanding federal powers, and unlike Cleveland, who was notorious for his dislike of government spending, Harrison supported a billion dollar appropriations bill in Congress, the largest such bill ever levied in peacetime. He also signed the Sherman Antitrust Act, which imposed unprecedented government regulations on the formation of monopolies and trusts; this marked a turning point in American history, the beginning of the era in which the federal government closely monitors the dealings of major corporations. Harrison was also one of the first presidents to take a strong interest in conserving American forests, which would eventually lead to the national parks movement. During Harrison's administration, the United States became, for the first time, a more active participant in global affairs, negotiating with the governments of Germany and Britain to acquire protectorates in the Samoan Islands. Benjamin Harrison was also the first president to advocate for the annexation of Hawaii as a state, though Hawaii would not be admitted to the Union until 1959.

Harrison ran for re-election in 1892, but several factors conspired against him, among them the fact that his wife, Caroline, was suffering from a terminal case of tuberculosis, which occupied most of his energy and attention. Former president Grover Cleveland ran as the Democratic candidate, and due to Caroline Harrison's illness, chose not to campaign against Harrison in public. Caroline Harrison died two weeks before Cleveland defeated Harrison in a decisive electoral victory of 145 to 277 votes. Upon the conclusion of his term, Harrison returned to Indiana to resume his law practice. In 1895, Harrison was married to his second wife, Mary Lord Dimmick, who was Caroline Harrison's niece and had been her nurse during the final stages of her illness. Nine years after the end of his presidency, Harrison died of pneumonia on March 13, 1901, at the age of 67. He was buried in Indianapolis, next to Caroline.

Memorable quote:

"The colored people did not intrude themselves upon us; they were brought here in chains and held in communities where they are now chiefly bound by a cruel slave code...when and under what conditions is the black man to have a free ballot? When is he in fact to have those full civil rights which have so long been his in law? When is that quality of influence which our form of government was intended to secure to the electors to be restored? ... in many parts of our country where the colored population is large the people of that race are by various devices deprived of any effective exercise of their political rights and of many of their civil rights. The wrong does not expend itself upon those whose votes are suppressed. Every constituency in the Union is wronged."

--President Benjamin Harrison, from an 1889 address to Congress regarding the Federal Elections Bill

Other great books by Michael W. Simmons on Kindle, paperback and audio:

Elizabeth I: Legendary Queen Of England

Alexander Hamilton: First Architect Of The American Government

William Shakespeare: An Intimate Look Into The Life Of The Most Brilliant Writer In The History Of The English Language

Thomas Edison: American Inventor

Catherine the Great: Last Empress of Russia

Romanov: The Last Tsarist Dynasty

Peter the Great: Autocrat and Reformer

The Rothschilds: The Dynasty and the Legacy

Queen Victoria: Icon of an Era

Six Wives: The Women Who Married, Lived, and
Died for Henry VIII

John D. Rockefeller: The Wealthiest Man in
American History

Princess to Queen: The Early Years of Queen
Elizabeth II

Queen of People's Hearts: The Life and Mission
of Diana, Princess of Wales

Jackie Kennedy Onassis: The Widow of Camelot

Ulysses S. Grant: The War Years

Marie Antoinette: Reversal of Fortune

Mary, Queen of Scots: White Queen, Red Queen

Further Reading

One: George Washington

Washington: A Life, by Ron Chernow

https://www.britannica.com/biography/George-Washington/Presidency

Two: John Adams

John Adams, by David McCullough

http://www.sparknotes.com/biography/johnadams/summary.html

Three: Thomas Jefferson

The Hemingses of Monticello, by Annette Gordon-Reed

Thomas Jefferson: the Art of Power, by Jon Meacham

http://www.history.com/topics/us-presidents/thomas-jefferson

Four: James Madison

James Madison: A Biography, by Ralph Ketcham

http://www.history.com/topics/us-presidents/james-madison

Five: James Monroe

The Last Founding Father: James Monroe and a Nation's Call to Greatness, by Harlow Giles Unger

https://millercenter.org/president/monroe/life-in-brief

Six: John Quincy Adams

John Quincy Adams (The American Presidents Series), by Robert V. Remini

https://www.biography.com/people/john-quincy-adams-9175983

Seven: Andrew Jackson

American Lion: Andrew Jackson in the White House, by Jon Meacham

http://www.historynet.com/andrew-jackson

Eight: Martin Van Buren

Martin Van Buren: The Romantic Age of American Politics, by John Niven

https://www.biography.com/people/martin-van-buren-9515025

Nine: William Henry Harrison

Old Tippecanoe: William Henry Harrison and His Times, by Freeman Cleaves

http://www.history.com/topics/us-presidents/william-henry-harrison

Ten: John Tyler

John Tyler: Champion of the Old South, by Oliver P. Chitwood

http://www.history.com/topics/us-presidents/john-tyler

Eleven: James Polk

The Man Who Transformed the Presidency and America, by Walter R. Borneman https://www.biography.com/people/james-polk-9443616

Twelve: Zachary Taylor

Zachary Taylor: Soldier, Planter, Statesman of the Old Southwest, by K. Jack Bauer

https://www.biography.com/people/zachary-taylor-9503363

Thirteen: Millard Fillmore

Millard Fillmore: Biography of a President, by Robert J. Rayback

http://www.history.com/topics/us-presidents/millard-fillmore

Fourteen: Franklin Pierce

Franklin Pierce (The American Presidents Series), by Michael Holt.

http://www.history.com/topics/us-presidents/franklin-pierce

Fifteen: James Buchanan

President James Buchanan: A Biography, by Philip S. Klein

http://www.history.com/topics/us-presidents/james-buchanan

Sixteen: Abraham Lincoln

Team of Rivals, by Doris Kearns Goodwin

Abraham Lincoln, by Michael Burlingame

http://www.historynet.com/abraham-lincoln

Seventeen: Andrew Johnson

Andrew Johnson (The American Presidents Series), by Annette Gordon-Reed

https://www.biography.com/people/andrew-johnson-9355722

Eighteen: Ulysses S. Grant

Grant, by Jean Edward Smith

http://www.historynet.com/ulysses-s-grant

Nineteen: Rutherford B. Hayes

Rutherford B. Hayes, and his America, by Harry Barnard

http://www.history.com/topics/us-presidents/rutherford-b-hayes

Twenty: James Garfield

Destiny of the Republic: A Tale of Madness, Medicine and the Murder of a President, by Candice Millard

https://www.biography.com/people/james-garfield-9306645

Twenty-One: Chester A. Arthur

Gentleman Boss: The Life of Chester Alan Arthur, by Thomas C. Reeves.

http://www.history.com/topics/us-presidents/chester-a-arthur

Twenty-Two and Twenty-Four: Grover Cleveland

Grover Cleveland: A Study in Character, by Alyn Brodsky

http://www.history.com/topics/us-presidents/grover-cleveland

Twenty-Three: Benjamin Harrison

Benjamin Harrison: Hoosier Statesman, by Harry Joseph Sievers

http://www.history.com/topics/us-presidents/benjamin-harrison

79130229R00151

Made in the USA
San Bernardino, CA
12 June 2018